AMERICAN WILD

Alternately profound, funny, and enlightening, Engelhard manages something rarely even attempted in outdoor literature: stories focused not on the death-defying prowess of the adventurer, but on the wild glory of place.

> —ERIN MCKITTRICK, author of *Small Feet Big Land* and *A Long Trek Home*

Michael Engelhard's beautifully crafted book, dedicated to opposing lands of extremes, is an intricate weaving of poetic language and luscious imagery, of reverence and outrage, of intellect, humor, and wit. At times a Zen-like docent of the land, at others a curmudgeonly sage in the Abbey tradition, Engelhard doesn't just show you around the wild places he hopelessly loves, he takes you deep into their souls, sharing the senses they evoke and the ancient stories embedded within.

> —DEBRA MCKINNEY, co-author of *Beyond the Bear*

As someone who spends her year commuting between these same two regions, I can think of no better ambassador for them than Michael Engelhard. Landscapes like these deserve such prose. Engelhard skillfully examines the threads that bind us to the land and reminds us how important it is that we protect these last wild places.

> —CHRISTA SADLER, editor of *There's This River* and author of *Life in Stone*

Michael Engelhard migrates like the thrushes we northerners so envy in autumn. This has given him a perspective of rare insight. Here, he takes us with him and we are richer for the journey.

> —NED ROZELL, author of *Finding Mars* and *Alaska Tracks*

With its exquisitely tough elegance and accordion range, Engelhard's prose growls and sings, appropriate for a writer whose twin poles of geographic passion are the Arctic and Southwest. Read him slowly, at the speed you would appreciate any array of delights, so as not to miss one fluting wren, deftly sketched fellow traveler, or diving grebe leaving "haiku pond-ripples." You will come away more ready to observe deeply and joyfully, more apt to draw thoughtful connections between your experiences and the natural world, and with a more nuanced insight into the dangers we pose to the places we love.

> —CAROL HARALSON, editor of *Sojourns* (Peaks, Plateaus & Canyons Association)

American Wild is a treasure—both for its agile and heartfelt prose and for the wild places, adventures, and people chronicled. Engelhard channels the soul of a philosopher through the heart of an untamed beast. He is an adventurer at home in diverse environs and respectful of gifts given, whether his hands grip paddle or pen, ice axe or potsherd.

> —STEVE KAHN, author of *The Hard Way Home*

With the assurance of one who is at home in wilderness, Engelhard weaves together his inner, emotional landscape and the outer, natural world. What emerges is the portrait of a man comforted and enlivened by what some would call the most harsh and inhospitable of places.

> —LAURIE HOYLE, co-author of *Arctic Sanctuary*

The wilderness needs a voice like Michael Engelhard—one that hums with honesty, lyricism, and sheer daring. In *American Wild*, he takes the reader on journeys where the gritty meets the ethereal. His spiritual reverence for the natural world radiates underneath careful language, and wonder flourishes with each turn of the page. It's a title fit for fans of nature writing that is at turns sharp, humorous, and moving.

> —SETH MULLER, editor of *Northern Arizona's Mountain Living Magazine*

American Wild

AMERICAN
WILD

*Explorations from the Grand Canyon
to the Arctic Ocean*

MICHAEL ENGELHARD

HIRAETH PRESS
DANVERS, MASSACHUSETTS

Front and back cover photographs by Melissa Guy
Author photograph by Melissa Guy
Cover and text design by Jason Kirkey

ISBN 978-0-9889430-9-4
First Edition 2016

Hiraeth Press books may be purchased for education, business or sale promotional use. For information, please write:

Special Markets
Hiraeth Press
P. O. Box 1442
Pawcatuck, CT 06379-1968

HIRAETH PRESS

DANVERS, MASSACHUSETTS
www.hiraethpress.com

❦ Hiraeth Press is a publisher with a mission. We are passionate about poetry as a means of returning the human voice to the chorus of the wild.

OH, GIVE ME A HOME where the muskoxen roam
Where the wolf and the caribou play,
Where seldom is heard a liberal's word,
And the sky is not smoggy and gray.

Where the air is so pure, the soul is so free,
The breezes so poignant and light,
That I would not exchange my homes on the range
For all of the cities so bright.

I love the wild flowers in this bright land of ours,
I love the wild loon's lonely keen,
The bluffs and red rocks, and bighorn sheep flocks
That graze on the riverbanks green.

Oh, give me the gleam of the whitewater stream
And the place where fierce dust devils blow;
Oh, give me the park where the ground squirrels bark
And the mountain all covered with snow.

Oh, give me the hills ringed with drab timber mills
And the poisonous ore in the ground;
Yes, give me the gulch where the miner can sluice
And the bright, yellow gold can be found.

Yes, give me a home where developers roam
Their business is always alive
In these backcountry hills midst the din of the drills
Oh, there let me live till I die.

—Adapted from Brewster M. Higley's 1872 poem
   My Western Home, which became the American
   West's unofficial anthem

Contents

Homes on the Range

IN THE YEAR I WAS BORN, tunnels blasted through Glen Canyon's cliffs opened to divert the Colorado River and allow dam construction to begin, which doomed that canyon and dozens of tributaries to flooding. Less than three months later, a bill was drafted for an Arctic National Wildlife Range, marking the first time in American history that politicians proposed federal protection for an entire ecosystem. Two decades after the bill's passage, the "range" was enlarged and renamed a "refuge," strengthening our society's message that some places should remain inviolate. My ongoing fascination with Glen Canyon and the Arctic Refuge, and by extension the Colorado Plateau and Alaska, owes much to the dynamics these two places represent: the conflict between hubris and awe, between greed and restraint, between myopia and conservationist vision.

"Fascination" I must quickly add, is such a lazy catchall for what runs much deeper. You can choose your region but not your character, a fan of the desert once wrote. But for some people character *dictates* the choice of a homeland, which in turn keeps rewriting their personality.

I firmly believe there are landscapes that speak to certain individuals more than others do, even to the extent where only one place ever makes a perfect match for such a person. A first exposure to this "soulscape" feels like a homecoming. Fortunately, I have found not one, but two. Unfortunately, lying 2,500 miles apart, they have sentenced me to a lifetime of wandering. Forced to choose, I would not know how to or which. Both remain jealous contenders for "that wedding of a writer and a region from which no divorce is possible." Call me a bigamist, if you like.

In truth, I am rather faithful to places, a bit of a homebody really, as I no longer venture outside my two preferred regions. There is precedence in nature for this. Some migratory species use the same stopovers, staging points, and breeding and wintering grounds year after year. The explanation is simple: these animals go where their needs are met best.

For somebody handy with words but handicapped when it comes to numbers, it is not always easy to peg dates—or even years—to particular memories. Among my abodes I've counted an oven-hot bunkhouse with slickrock views, an unheated sauna near the Arctic Circle, a houseboat parked on a ranch in British Columbia, a survivalist bunker-home in a bentonite hill, and a blue-tarp hut shaped like a Tootsie Roll on the banks of the Rio Grande. The chronology can get muddled, and I often resort to my journals or resume to sort it out. For the past twenty-five years, I've spun my life between two different but in many ways similar worlds. My bearings forever pointed me north and southwest. Fairbanks and Moab have been base camps repeatedly, lode points for my peregrinations; Tatlayoko, Lajitas, Terlingua, Elfrida, Arroyo Seco, Oracle, Moran Junction, Flagstaff, Whitehorse, Nome, and most recently Cordova, have been way stations, bivouacs in a manner of speaking. Over the years, the scope of my desire has narrowed, centering on the

Four Corners' high desert and America's Farthest North. I've been gravitating between these two regions like tides pulled by the moon, though commuting for guiding work to Alaska when I lived in the desert and vice versa only complicated matters. Craving novelty as a younger man, I'd wanted to climb a thousand different mountains, to flee, in the words of the philosopher Frédéric Gros, "the sordid idiocies of the sated ones." Now, as in the Chinese proverb, I wanted to climb the same mountain a thousand times to learn all I could—how it looked in different seasons and angles of light; how it sounded and smelled; the creatures and plants it hosted; how it and I fit in with the rest. For the longest time, the muddy Y of the Colorado and Green River confluence had me enthralled. It was the closest an agnostic pilgrim could ever come to finding a shrine. My email handle, nedludinmoab, perfectly situated and suited me, though it smacked a bit of surrender. I *was* a Luddite in redrock country. I had not driven since the Army made me, did not wear a watch, or have a phone; the most complex gadget I owned was a backpacking stove.

My refusal to gather moss acknowledged what Jared Diamond calls "The Worst Mistake in the History of the Race." Our settling from hunter-gatherer ways into soil-tilling drudgery deserves the comparison with Pandora's box. It sprang on us Civilization's surprises, from systemic warfare to social hierarchies and pandemics. Footloose Neanderthals did not get heart attacks, Alzheimer's, or anemia, did not feel ennui or alienated at work. They paid no parking tickets or taxes.

Regrettably, progress, or what commonly passes for progress, has a way of leaving places I've come to love compromised. I try in vain to outrun development. Why do I sometimes return? Memory is a doddering fool, and mine keeps romancing the past and the spatially faraway. I should have long ago heeded Aldo Leopold's advice to never revisit old haunts. Moving on, or back, I often find the "lily of wilderness" has not been gilded—it has been tarnished, traded for trinkets or coarse cash. To a degree, Alaska still is what the West once was: untamed, abounding with space and large fauna and possibilities to avoid past mistakes. But on closer acquaintance, its frontier mentality, the motto "get rich quickly and get out," starts to grate.

The recurring urge to uproot myself, of course, is nothing but the old immigrant dream in disguise, the founding myth of a nation, the promise that somewhere beyond the horizon a better life is waiting. And as the record shows, those who pull up stakes once are likely to do so again. Unsurprisingly, a lot of this country's literature reflects such restlessness, from Huck Finn to Muir's rambles to Kerouac's *On the Road*. I've thus joined the ranks, as Scott Russell Sanders dismissively put it, "of earnest pilgrims, idle drifters, travelers who write from a distance about places they have abandoned, or nomads who write about no place at all." I offer these tales of my explorations hoping to show that the nomad's commitment to places, like that of the whale or crane, can match Thoreau's or Wendell Berry's in every way.

My continued hopscotching between two regions does not entirely owe to limp "the grass is always greener" sentiments; much of the time not much grass grows where I live. But the light is always more rarefied "there," the space less cluttered, the residents more unconventional, less worn-down by mundane concerns—at least until I've settled in again and begin to remember. Each change of perspective addictively re-sharpens my ability to perceive things anew. Long sightlines, the lack of dense forests or human populations, both in the Arctic and the Southwest set my heartstrings to humming. The pellucid, dry air deceives about distances, makes details and truths stand out like pebbles in a mountain stream. Nowhere else have I seen stars that seem within reach, let alone auroras' witchy tourmaline veils. Encounters with wolves, bighorns, rattlers, mountain lions, and grizzly bears leave me breathless and riveted to these places. Sounds and scents somehow carry farther here than they do elsewhere: river ice grinding during break-up, a canyon wren's fluting, cliffrose perfume, or the musk and old-man grunts of caribou all evoke half-buried, primal memories. Temperatures spiking at minus 60 and 110 degrees have tested my mettle, extremes that through climate and flora also shape scenery. Arctic and canyon landscapes can afford, and demand, patience. Neither needs to overwhelm with easy bucolic glitter. Absences largely define both. Mountains diminish visibly there; erosion scoops out gulches, gorges, arroyos, and glacial valleys—inverted ridges, negative space. Human noise seldom intrudes, or at least, used to. (You know it is quiet when you can hear your empty stomach complaining.) In high latitudes even daylight goes missing for part of the year. Stripped of the extraneous, these lands lie bared to all senses. In wind-scoured homesteads and tent rings of stones on the tundra, those who once lived there left palpable voids. With few exceptions, wildlife is secretive, seasonally scarce, and most often revealed only in the signs of its passing. Unruffled by lush plant life or built structures, the mind can latch on to geology, which, far from being static, betrays entropy at a pace and scale that challenges comprehension. As a constant reminder of mortality—I weigh my life span against the eons—the topographic breakdown highlights moments more vividly, providing relief. In more than just literal ways, the desert and Arctic, if you can love them, will widen your horizons. Perhaps most importantly, both retain some of the best America has to offer: room for us and other creatures to breathe or disappear.

These topographies may rank among North America's harshest and most exacting, but what a landscape asks of you and what it offers in turn sometimes balances finely.

There is also, impossible to ignore, my affinity for the two regions' aboriginal cultures, for their worldviews and ways of being in the world. I easily identify with the traditional nomadism of Alaska's Koyukon and Gwich'in Indians and Inupiaq Eskimos—about whom I first read in undergraduate classes—and with that of their southern cousins, the Navajos and Apaches. The more sedentary Hopi claim a place in my heart simply because they were the first Native people that took me in, during my first sojourn in the Southwest. Their cliff-dwelling ancestors left traces I never tire exploring, mysteries I hope will never be solved.

Anthropologists have been accused of discontent with their own culture. As a tribe, almost by definition, they value the underdog. I have always rooted for Manuelito over Kit Carson, for coyotes over Chihuahuas, for Trickster over the trinity, black widows over Black Diamond. That contrast to me is the essence of these American wilds. Too much Jack London during my adolescence and too much Ed Abbey during later but no less formative years may have confounded my problem. As far back as I can remember, dissatisfaction with cities and homesickness for lands labeled "austere" clouded my days. I am a fence sitter, a vagrant by inclination and training, and this vantage serves my writing equally well.

Southwest

Every man, every woman, carries in heart and mind the image of the ideal place, the right place, the one true home, known or unknown, actual or visionary.

—EDWARD ABBEY, *Desert Solitaire* (1968)

No Walk in the Park

> You cannot see the Grand Canyon in one view, as if it were
> a changeless spectacle from which a curtain might be lifted,
> but to see it you have to toil from month to month through
> its labyrinths. It's a region more difficult to traverse than the
> Alps or the Himalayas....
>
> —JOHN WESLEY POWELL, *The Exploration of the Colorado
> River and Its Canyons* (1874)

I WAS ON MY THIRD PAIR OF BOOTS, my second pair of shorts,
and my air mattress was leaking—the canyon's abrasiveness
had taken its toll. Ravens had hacked into my clear-plastic water
bladder, thinking perhaps that its content was gin. I had busted a
hiking pole and lost a lens from my sunglasses when a wind gust
skittered them off a Redwall Limestone rock bench, stranding
them three stories below. My hiking bud Andrew, a herpetologist
built like a fire hydrant, swarthy of looks, choleric of temper,
bull-headed as myself, had climbed down a rock chimney to
retrieve the now useless eyewear. At the same camp, a custard-
colored scorpion scuttled from my ground cloth when I folded
it up in the morning.

Somewhere on the high saddles route, Andrew's camera got yanked off when we lowered our packs with a rope. His bargain sombrero had frayed the first day, and he now wore a bandana headband-style. His shirt hung in tatters, reinforcing his Rambo appearance. The shirt was a precious memento. He'd worn it on trips with his wife, who fell to her death from these Redwall cliffs less than two years before. Our intended seventy-day through-hike—largely off-trail, on the canyon's north side—in part sought to honor her, her short life, her zest for adventure, her dream of walking the length of this gorge. Introduced by an acquaintance, Andrew and I had hiked for four days together the previous spring, to check our compatibility. We were both spellbound by long quests in this convoluted yet simple place, an obsession we shared with certain math teachers, photographers, backcountry rangers, canyon historians, and river rats. Some had paid dearly, gone missing or drowned by wretched flash floods. One self-destructed after hiking both sides of the canyon, unable to cope with reentry into what people kept calling "the real world." Here, the view alone could kill. When first exposed to it, a tourist at Yaki Point fainted and toppled 500 feet to end up looking like a rag doll.

The abyss stared into us and we into it.

It did not spare our bodies either. Blackbrush, locust, agaves, and carnivorous limestone gouged my forearms and shins. (I was saving my long pants for the cool days ahead.) My knees and lower back ached, embedded spines festered, and the pack's hip belt left plum-colored bruises. My boots' narrow toe-box pinched like Chinese foot-binding. A gash running from Andrew's elbow to his wrist, from a wipeout on an unstable stone slab, had barely begun to scab.

Some stretches along the river resembled a booby-trapped jungle gym. Precariously balanced, cabin-size rocks alternated with tamarisk thickets and snarls of mesquite and aptly named catclaw acacia. On the canyon's Tonto Platform shoulder, extensive prickly pear forced us to high-step as through a minefield. We got rattled at a few times, but mostly, with winter pending, the buzzworms were lethargic. The midges that on some days drove Andrew buggy did not bother me much. I've had worse, in Alaska.

Once in a while, rewards for our workouts came in the form of full, peeling beer cans, "river booty" from the bags that rafts dragged to keep drinks cold, which we fished from driftwood-clogged bays. The beers were lukewarm, and I've seldom had better. One that Andrew was saving for dinner in the outside mesh-pocket of his pack got punctured when he put down his load. I still smile at the memory of him sucking beer suds spraying from the hole, cursing between sips.

The four kinds of dehydrated pouch-dinner I carried never got old though the bloating they caused quickly did. We looked forward to mashed potatoes or Pad Thai as if they were four-star cuisine. "Mi-so happy," Andrew would pidgin-crow, slurping Japanese instant soup like Buddha on a rolled-out sleeping bag.

Just when the weight of our packs was getting bearable, we'd reach one of our food caches; fully loaded again, we felt as if gravity had doubled overnight. Despite meals that could fatten a galley slave and treats guest hikers delivered (salami and cheese; oranges; a half-gallon of vanilla ice cream on dry ice) our waistlines receded. The midnight snack in the sleeping bag had become routine. Our beards, meanwhile, were filling in lavishly, streaked silver-gray. We rinsed our T-shirts and socks in potholes or eddies whenever we could but nevertheless looked feral and smelled like ringtails in heat.

We enjoyed some luxuries at Teddy's Cabin on Bass Canyon's Muav Saddle, one of the few huts in the "Big Ditch." Laying over there for a day, we carried water up from the spring to do laundry, and I dashed to the rim for a six-pack of beer visiting hikers had promised to leave for us. Worried about rodent-borne hantavirus and by now used to sleeping under the stars, I moved one bedframe outside, where the wind swished through feathery ponderosa boughs all night long. Dreaming among waltzing trees was as good as dreaming rocked by the river's waves on a raft 5,000 feet below. There too, I've felt connected to a huge vascular system, buoyed by its heaving, its breathing. And waking up to sunlight kissing pine tops or cliffs simply is priceless.

Most days, though, we hopped boulders, traversed talus, spread-eagled through limestone maws, edge-walked, bush-whacked, switch-backed, stream-waded, scrambled, thirsted, and pined for our girlfriends—mine luckily joined us at South Canyon for two weeks. We struggled on each geological layer between the river and rim, from the yellow-gray Toroweap to the black, brooding, titanic Vishnu schist. We cautiously shuffled along the chasm's brink, sometimes on treacherous ball-bearings gravel, going where even bighorn sheep fear to tread. When we were hauling up water with a rope from a pothole to which we had to rappel, a hardcore, visiting canyoneer tore a tendon. That put him out of commission for close to a year. We had his number and in tight spots called him on the satellite phone for route information or replacement gear. But at least we'd avoided a full-blown search and rescue—for now. "No news is good news," we had briefed our safety contact in Phoenix.

We had been rather fortunate with the weather. Some of the blistering heat we eased by soaking bandanas and T-shirts and by joining lizards under their rocks when the sun beat down most brutally. In a few places, water-pockets or springs we had counted on greeted us dusty and barren. Elsewhere, we left the river for a better route higher up, but long, chalk-dry miles convinced us that hiking onshore wasn't so bad after all. Cliffs often kept us from the vital fluid when we changed our minds and wanted to descend.

I particularly remember the afternoon, when, after a long day on the Redwall rim, we dropped into Rider Canyon near the sweet beach at House Rock Rapid, the day's destination. A huge natural stone-table by the stream there—the "House Rock

Hotel"—promised respite with cool breezes. Our water bottles were empty, my face was burning, the smooth sandstone baking, and the death-star hung overhead, torturing flesh and ringing like a giant brass gong. When we finally reached the river, I dove into its emerald curl as into a lover's embrace.

The potholes had been refilled in late August, just in time for our hike, by a series of gully-washers that had scoured the North Rim. An ultra-light backpacking shelter I'd decorated with my totem—a carefully painted bear-paw print—turned out to be overpriced junk. During a deluge at Clear Creek, it collected a half-inch of rain in its Silicon tub-bottom. Squalls had roared through the gorge all night long, caged beasts that threatened to drop cottonwood "widow makers" on our pup tents. By morning, snow filigreed the South Rim's upper layers. My gear and sleeping bag were sopping wet. Another time we bedded down in an alcove, in the dust of millennia, watched over by painted sheep and Miró-style shaman figures, while drizzle glazed the canyon floor outside of our chamber. We also nearly got lost in a sand storm on our return to camp after dinner with river runners below Nankoweap Rapid. Our headlamps had stabbed the night like pale fingers as we tipsily wove through the washes, spotlighting ghost bushes and cliff faces confusing in their sameness.

That was it, as far as vagaries of weather were concerned—the rest of our days shone robin-egg blue, shimmering uniformly, luscious pearls on a string.

We did, however, ride out a perfect bureaucratic storm: the park shutdown, result of the stalemate over the federal budget. I first heard about it through Andrew's inReach, a satellite-serviced texting and GPS device. Rumors circulated that rangers would intercept us or detain us at Phantom Ranch, where we had placed a cache, and escort us out. Because Andrew posted our whereabouts daily, they would know where to find us, just as they would radio-collared sheep.

Downstream of East Clear Creek, we noticed signs of abandonment. No more river trips passed us; trails and campsites lay vacant. Descending through the stacked-deck Tapeats Sandstone, we could not see any hikers or mules on the South Kaibab Trail. The gossamer footbridge across the river linked to a beach and corrals, to a campground, lodge, and guest cabins, all eerily silent. Had I not known about the shutdown, I might have suspected a new 9/11 or mysterious plague. Word finally reached us, as digital text, that after a high-echelon meeting, the Park Service decided to let us continue, consistent with its treatment of river runners who were allowed to proceed if they had launched before the closure. Suspicious by nature, I still was prepared to sneak onto the ranger cabin's porch to grab my rodent-proof food bucket under the cover of darkness.

I need not to have worried. The ranger on duty released our supplies and told us we could pick any campsite. The Park Service had even made arrangements to bring in my replacement boots and Andrew's cold weather gear with the last mule train to leave the South Rim. It was "a safety issue," after all. With Townes Van Zandt moaning from Andrew's iPhone, we sipped single malt whiskey at the campground's group site at a picnic table close to a bathroom with water taps and electric outlets, but the post-apocalyptic vibe lingered. What a rare, historical moment. We were the sole visitors in the normally busy inner gorge, holdouts on closed public lands. We were the last legal hikers within 2,000 square miles. When I saw off my girlfriend at the downstream suspension bridge, it felt like a scene from *The Road*.

Things started coming apart between Andrew and me on day thirty-eight, things that could not be fixed with our well-stocked repair kit. I could blame clashing views about culture, about science, the outdoors but ultimately, it was personalities. Like some old couple, we knew where to aim knife-words to draw blood. It was as if the canyon's prickliness had rubbed off on us. One blowup happened when Andrew mocked Hopi creation myths and I in turn, needling, called evolution the creation myth of biologists. But what bothered me most was the white noise of civilization, which Andrew carried in his pack, the electronic chatter asserting itself day and night to the point of distraction. I was with Mark Twain who, apropos of the newly invented telephone, quipped that the human voice carries entirely too far as it is.

With sat phone, iPhone, and inReach, Andrew tried to stay updated, yoked to his city existence. Though some messages clearly upset him, he'd respond to texts, sometimes while on foot. The inReach's green eye watched over his sleep; I watched the coursing of satellites that kept us ensnared. When, at the crux of a climb through the Redwall, the inReach in Andrew's pack began chirping, a line between here and back home had been rudely breached. "You cannot escape from your life," Andrew had said—but I just wanted a break from it. I wished for a few weeks to concentrate only on this barebones place, to absorb its air of splendid isolation. Like the curmudgeonly Edward Abbey, I found my contemplation of nature compromised when too many people were contemplating it with me at the same time. I had come for the silence and "silences," those spaces on maps, ever more rare, left blank by cartographers. I welcomed guest hikers for their contributions to our larder, less so for the news they brought of the outside world. With each contact with new people, the dynamics subtly shifted; there was never a sense of cohesion, of a core of friends that grew closer with the miles they traversed. Each social shake-up felt like another throw of the dice. Just when I got used to visitors, it was time for them to leave.

Andrew, conversely, enjoying new people, hailed each passing trip, even from the Redwall a thousand feet above river level, and visited every camp, loitering in the kitchen area, hoping for dinner or company or a pat on the head.

I cannot say in good conscience that the chronic dehydration from which we both suffered had nothing to do with our crabbiness. (Despite expert advice to drink enough water for my urine to flow "clear and copious," I never managed to do so on the trip.) But neither can brains that had shrunk into dried figs serve as an adequate excuse.

After one more argument, we parted ways at an alcove with six-foot skeletal ghosts painted on its ceiling. I pulled out the climbing gear I had carried and told Andrew I was leaving. I nearly had run out of food—we were going to pick up cache number seven the next day near the rim. The route up there was not straightforward, marked only on the map inside Andrew's pack. Too proud to ask for a look at it, I shouldered my load and took off.

An hour later, cornered by bulging Supai Sandstone, I conceded that I was off-course. Rather than risk falling or wasting more daylight, I decided to exit the long way, at the Tuckup Canyon trailhead. Unfortunately, at this time of year, there might be no traffic on the spur dirt road leaving that canyon. The best option for catching a ride required a sixteen-mile walk from Tuckup to the Toroweap Road.

My final dinner under the stars consisted of a snack bar and orange fizzy drink.

The next morning, before dawn enflamed the Dome, I was climbing switchbacks to the trailhead. From there, I followed the rutted track that rolled through piñon-juniper forest and sage flats. My empty belly protested but I was not quite ready to quaff olive oil, the only calories left in my pack.

Eternities later, after trudging on autopilot with daydreams of pizza and cheesecake, I approached the corral near the Toroweap Road. Two pickups and a Polaris—an ATV on steroids masquerading as golf cart—were parked there. Perhaps these belonged to hunters or ranchers, with whom I could ride to Fredonia.

As I drew closer, to my surprise, I saw the Toroweap ranger perched on the ATV's roof, radio and map in hand.

"There he is," said one of the guys by the pickups. It was our go-to canyoneer, who had helped place our cache and who'd met Andrew there this morning. When they realized that my food bucket had not been touched, they'd grown concerned and talked to the ranger, who happened to be there for a routine check. He was just about to call for a search-and-rescue helicopter when I sauntered up. Even when I thought I'd escaped, I never slipped the dragnet net in the ether.

Back home for hibernation—my scratches and blisters mend nicely, and I'm putting on pounds. I briefly ponder how wilderness brings out the best and the worst in us, how the desert glare throws flaws and passions into relief as no other light does. How it asks that you surrender your self without guarantee of returns. Then, bent over maps, already forgetting, I start planning my next walk in a park.

A River Now and Again

WHEN WE EXIT THE TRUCK, applause greets us, ringing frenetically from the Little Colorado River gorge. Near the overlook, it swells to a crescendo, a roar with a booming bass note, foot stomping in the bleachers. The streambed and Grand Falls, which lies barren or reduced to a runnel for most of the year, have sprung back to life.

Thrilled by the high-flow levels the United States Geological Survey posted online we drove two hours from Flagstaff, on paved byways, across reservation washboard, through pine woods, and past volcanic cinder cones, with not a drop of water in sight. Time passed quickly as we chatted and hashed out the logistics of shuttling cars between the put-in and takeout.

At the overlook, speechless, we face a mirage: an off-color Niagara in the desert.

Gravity rules at the lip, while farther down, the canyon-cutter writhes like a coral pink, glossy worm. Cascades leap from the falls' outer edges. The main current charges with biblical force over tiered, beveled limestone ledges midstream. Falling, it unravels in frothed dizziness, forming massive, ragged jets. It would be a feat to track any flotsam after it slips off the brink. Bloated to an eddying lake, the plunge pool at the bottom trembles with chop but calms near the outlet. Water vaporizes in the impact zone, lashing tamarisks on shore. Driftwood carpets a beach in the cove; more spins on its flood in a miniature logjam, enough to build pyres or rafts.

Innocent and incongruent, a thin, blue sky arcs above everything. I shudder as much from the spectacle as from the sharp March air, expecting to feel vibrations through the soles of my feet.

Grand Falls is not just a quirk of hydrology but also one of geology. Some 20,000 years ago, lava from a vent known as The Sproul oozed across the flats and into the Little Colorado's trough, plugging it with a basalt dam. The river was forced to detour, spilling over the dam, and Grand Falls was born.

At 185 feet, the falls stand twenty feet taller than Niagara. Their range of moods illustrates that a river at heart is a weather phenomenon. In droughts, there is not enough flow to buoy a duck. In flood, the wash channels run off from monsoon cloudbursts or snowmelt from Arizona's White Mountains, near the New Mexico state line. A good portion of the Painted Desert— friable siltstone, sandstone, and clay—ends up rebuilding eroded beaches in the Grand Canyon.

The Spanish missionary Francisco Garcés called it Rio Jaquesila—the "River Unruly." The Navajos called it Red Water. A river *muy macho*, *muy colorado*, indeed. The men on John Wesley Powell's first expedition deemed it "so filthy and muddy that it fairly stinks." They guessed half of its volume and two thirds of its weight to be muddy silt. It could carry worse things, however, and it has. In 1979, in the biggest radioactive spill in U. S. history, 100 million gallons of waste slopped from the tailings pond of United Nuclear Corporation's Church Rock uranium mill into the Puerco River, an upper fork of the watershed. Toxic sludge reached the Navajo reservation, where traces can still be detected today. Children played in ephemeral, pus-yellow puddles, and elders who waded the river to gather their sheep lost their legs later or died from the hellish effluent's burn. This legacy may seem remote in space and time, but as the biologist and cancer survivor Sandra Steingraber reminds us, we all live downstream of some headwater. Just open a tap in your kitchen for proof.

In drier conditions the lower Little Colorado runs shallow and leisurely, in no great rush to join the main stream. Laced with minerals from pulsing Blue Spring, it glows like Curaçao liqueur near its Grand Canyon confluence with the Colorado. The Mormons and other settlers had difficulties crossing it even in its mellow state. Their teams and wagons often bogged down in quicksand. It was easier to ford at Grand Falls and the smaller Black Falls, ten miles below, where the river slides over bedrock.

The initial spell has broken. Shouting above the din, we point and laugh and shake our heads in disbelief. My girlfriend, Melissa, who stands next to me, works as a public health nurse and visits homesteads throughout this part of the Navajo reservation, routinely driving across just upstream of here, sometimes without wetting the truck's tires. Were she to try today, she would get swept to her death. At the flow gauge near Cameron, the river registered almost six feet deep, passing more than the load of a twenty-foot freight container every second.

A half-mile long trail winds steeply into the seething cauldron, and we hump down two Hypalon toys plus gear: paddles, daypacks, an air pump, and life jackets. Eager to launch, we inflate our kayaks on a sliver of beach. Christa and I are going to look at the chocolate-milk rush from up close. As a desert geologist and Grand Canyon raft guide she cannot resist its siren song, and neither can I. Melissa chooses to stay on shore, because we did not bring drysuits, and the spray looks as if it could drench you in a minute. For the same reason she decides to walk around the pool's outlet, a boulder-flanked funnel with a pour-over boiling in the middle—a Class II rapid, easily. She's always been smart about this sort of thing.

Christa and I sit ten yards from the monstrous wall, dabbling to keep our distance. We don't want to get pushed under it by the gyre; it would destroy our crafts. "The world is rough and surly," wrote Ralph Waldo Emerson, "and will not mind drowning a man or a woman." Or a man *and* a woman. Except for stampeding wildlife, few things in nature move with the mass and speed of a river in flood: clouds, twisters, avalanches, tsunamis.... But you can join none of these, or only at risk to life or limb. If you manage to do so, precarious empowerment is your reward. Still, to truly understand any river, you have to be in it, not on it. Spray blasts us, and my clothes begin to soak through. It is even chillier here, in the river's mist plume. Seen from this close, the falls seem to rotate horizontally, like a huge cylinder, causing moments of trance. The motion suggests a perpetual mobile; it's hard to imagine this silt conveyor could ever slow down, or stop.

When we've had our fill, we paddle toward the outlet. Christa runs it first. Not watching her line, not bracing, and not shifting my weight forward, I hit the center hole. The bow goes up and I go flying. Gasping from the rapid's punch, I swallow a sediment-laden pint—at this time of year, snowmelt from the high country feeds it. My kayak races ahead, upside-down, but I manage to hold on to the paddle.

In passing, I catch a glimpse of my girlfriend snapping candid shots from shore.

At this water level, there are few eddies to pull into. Luckily, Christa is parked in one with my ducky in tow. I crawl from the shallows winded and not quite clear yet what happened. I have to look at the pictures later to figure it out. Not anticipating a swim, I didn't dress for one. I begin to shiver immediately, with my teeth clacking castanet-style.

Meanwhile, Melissa has joined us, offering dry layers from her pack. My stuff is still there, strapped into the boat. But it's sopping, and I've lost my favorite ball cap. I'll now have to wear a girlie knit hat.

After a quick snack of trail mix and cheese—fuel for the faltering engine—we shove off, Christa in one boat, Melissa and I in the other. I'm shaking so hard that Melissa, in the front seat, feels the kayak vibrating.

Let the fun begin. With the river hushed between here and the landing, we hope to spice up adventure with a dash of archaeology.

Wet or dry, this gulch has attracted people for at least 11,000 years. Some Ice Age hunter lost a leaf-shaped, fluted spear point on the prairie close by, a fine blade for killing mammoths; the bones of one surfaced not far from here; the obsidian came from fifty miles away. The lower gorge enfolds the Sipapu, a travertine dome spring from which the Hopis climbed after three previous worlds had been destroyed. Cut loose from this umbilicus—their most recent place of origin—they were set adrift in the fourth and final world. After they settled down, the Little Colorado connected Homolovi and the Hopi Mesas to the north with Wupatki, the Grand Canyon, and points south. Goods, individuals, and ideas trickled both ways, according to season and want. Tokens of far-flung trade—Mexican copper bells and scarlet macaws, seashells from the Pacific—traveled as far as Wupatki. The hundred-room pueblo squats on a rock knoll near our takeout and the Black Falls Road, which crosses the river. Its Mesoamerican-type ball court is the northernmost of its kind. Between 500 and 1225 CE, when they permanently abandoned Wupatki, driven, most likely, by drought, thousands of people lived there or within a day's walk, in outliers such as Wukoki and The Citadel. At these bustling crossroads mingled Sinagua, Cohonina, and Kayenta Anasazi, ancestors of modern Puebloans. They pecked evidence of their beliefs and preoccupations into rock varnish alongside this river. It's an outdoor gallery hard to match, even on the rock-art rich Colorado Plateau.

I cannot get warm, despite wearing hat, gloves, and life jacket on our strolls to the petroglyphs. There are simply too many to check out each one if we want to make Wupatki before nightfall. Engraved in the cliffs' metallic skin are spiders, bears, turtles, bighorn sheep, birds, lizards, and joyous dancers. Flute players and "traders"—figures with packs and hiking sticks—march solo or single-file. A throw-dart sprouts from the back of one traveler, an ambush or act of revenge perhaps. I show Christa, a sworn cat lover, the glyph of an archer who aims at four felines. (Though they could well be rodents.) The animals seem to be tied together by their tails, pulling in directions that correspond to the four compass points. I tell Christa, whose cats to my dismay ever so often zap hummers at her birdfeeders, that I'll call this the Animal Control Panel. She does not think that is funny. In another scene, nine sheep have been speared with missiles launched by a throwing-board or *atlatl*. Each bend brings a new discovery. Against the red dirt, flint chips and potsherds with black-on-white lattices shine like bone scatter in the sun. We find hewn spirals, waves, sun and star patterns, lozenges, zigzags, and checkerboards that mirror ceramic or textile designs. We find psychedelic amoebas and cerebral mazes, hoof marks and footprints, archives embossed with lichen or crisp as new pennies. We find no watercraft, no swimmers, no sign that the ancient ones entrusted themselves to this shifty highway; but some scrawls might celebrate clan migrations, or the river's curved detours.

Biased, perhaps, by the shape of our journeys, we perceive rivers as finite, linear, stretched source-to-sea. We name their main stems, sections, and tributaries. We speak of waterlines, waterways, river left, river right, arteries, forks. We envision them vascular, muscular, serpentine, braided, branching, threading, or ribboning. We rank them by length and plot GPS points to cairn remote float trips for others to follow. Some people tally the rivers they've "done," sometimes in logbooks or lists. Others rhapsodize, praising them with story or song, with a fluency of their own.

To the naturalist John Graves, a river is, like a body, "one of the real wholes." But lines of our doing dissect rivers—dams, locks, and weirs, wheel ruts, bridges, and cables, pipelines and power lines, and invisibly, lines that split the liquid asset or "resource" between counties, between upper and lower basin states, lines that sever what should be inseverable, perhaps even sacred.

A Navajo ceremonial name for the Colorado, "Life Without End," imparts a deeper truth. Cyclical, dynamical, ephemeral, rivers fluctuate in space and time. They are channel surfers, opportunists, quick-change artists—topography's transients or mayflies. Rain or snow falls, gathers in rills, then rivulets, and rolls on, past confluences, into reservoirs, through deltas, to ocean shores, and into marine depths; it ascends and joins clouds, to be held as insurance against future shortages. And so on, ad infinitum. Every sixth grader knows this. Still we chart river-flow graphs, map bowknot bends. Circles and spirals much better encrypt the nature of water—any water. But we forget, viewing rivers as we view life: vectors to be gauged not miracles to be mulled.

It is getting late, and the gorge slowly wraps itself in shadows. Once in a while, the stream wells up a gurgle. In the deep quiet I hear paddles dripping and silt hissing against the tubes. Already the falls have become hearsay, unreal.

At our last stop we climb to ruins that stand on the north rim like broken teeth. Touched by the westering sun, tawny sandstone walls blush cinnabar. The river's abrading yields clay, the mortar that once kept these walls from crumbling. One building block bears a fossil imprint. The crocodile ancestor's three-lobed track lends to the ruin an aura of time beyond time, a time before humans were even so much as a thought in the mind of creation. There is permanence of a sort next to this *wadi*, this fickle flow that has channeled pilgrims and settlers, locals and travelers, a place that draws worshippers to this day.

Still cold, or cold again, I begin the descent to the boats. We've got a long way to go, and a portage around a diversion dam yet ahead. We'll be looping back to the truck at Grand Falls in the dark. But we don't mind. It's another day with the river, another circuit completed. At home, in our easy chairs, it will be good to remember that silt happens now and again.

Dancing the Rain

A DRUM STEADY AS A METRONOME announces the procession. The still February air buzzes with anticipation, and my goose bumps are not from the cold. I am packed shoulder to shoulder with raven-haired people on a flat roof in Muh-oon-qah-pi, the "Place of Running Water," waiting to fall out of time.

Owl hoots join the drum, and then hail on flagstones—rattling from deer hooves, seeds, turtle shells. Here they come! A crush of masked bodies daubed with the land's minerals, bright as hummingbirds, feathers and furs swaying, pounding bare ground with bare feet, inflating cloud bellows and bringing up seedlings with each stomp. This is Powamyua, the start of the Hopi ceremonial year and first appearance of the *katsina* spirits since their winter retreat to the San Francisco Peaks near Flagstaff.

I am in Moenkopi with a few river guides and Grand Canyon National Park staff as part of Northern Arizona University's Native Voices on the Colorado River. Through cultural immersion, this program seeks to increase our understanding of tribes affiliated with the canyon. Its practical goal is to enrich the interpretation of a cultural landscape by including First Peoples' perspectives.

Fortunately, we are not on our own. William Talashoma, a river guide and interpreter from Moenkopi, shepherds us through the maze of Hopi etiquette and beliefs. For a change, we guides are the guided ones, feeling like babes in the desert. On our way to the village, we briefly stopped at Cameron, near the lip of the Little Colorado River's gorge. There, William recounted his people's emergence from previous worlds, destroyed by ice, fire, and flood, into this present and final one. The place of emergence lies down canyon, near the confluence with the Colorado, where a travertine dome housing a spring swells from the riverbank like an earthen breast. Its Hopi name, Sipapuni, translates as "navel" or "umbilical cord." William thinks of it as symbolic, a reminder of rebirth and the fact that we come from the earth. It evokes our ascent from primordial muck to consciousness. Fittingly, the souls of the dead return to this gateway for their journey home. As a navigational landmark, the Sipapuni pegs the tribe's surfacing from the canyon's depths onto the mesa tops after epic migrations across the Southwest that followed its last emergence.

At Moenkopi, we parked our van bumper to bumper with cars by the side of a congested dirt road. Down that road, single-story houses huddled between tan bluffs and the wash's dormant cornfields. We followed a trickle of visitors toward the lower village, to the cottonwood-shaded spring that gave the village its name and still gives it life. Offerings had been left in a shrine-like niche: Turkey feathers tied with white cotton string. A broken rattle. Yellow cornmeal. Carved prayer sticks, both male and female kinds, painted turquoise. I stooped to pick up a gray, corrugated potsherd that could have been a thousand years old. Though Moenkopi only dates back to 1870, the Hopi's Motsinom ancestors probably worshipped there.

As portals to the spirit world, springs did and still do hold meaning for people of the corn.

We shared lunch with William's family, eating in shifts, as the house was bursting with guests. On the porch, a boy played with a painted bow, a gift from the *katsinas*. We sat at a lunch counter, where we were served *piki*—phyllo-thin blue corn bread baked on a fire-heated flat stone. A girl with almond eyes and a shy smile warned me of the batch spiced with chilies. There was fry bread and beef soup with bean sprouts grown for the occasion in the underground secrecy of kivas, the clans' ceremonial chambers. The Powamyua or "Bean Dance" concludes a sixteen-day ceremony of creation. The elemental spirits or *katsinas* have arrived in force, helping the Hopi prepare for the growing season and, if the rites are performed humbly and correctly, will bring rain from the sacred peaks to the south. It also marks the initiation of young children into the entry-level Katsina Society, preparing yet another generation for growth and maturity.

Laughter erupted from the table around which elders and close family sat. In a dimly lit corner, an old-timer with mahogany skin reclined in a hospital bed, part of the proceedings.

Like the planet's progress solemnized here, my journeying has come full circle. New to the country, I was hitchhiking across the Southwest in 1983 when a Hopi who offered a ride invited me to visit with his family on Third Mesa. I stayed at his grandmother's house for a few days. A potter from the renowned Nampeyo lineage, she fired pots the traditional way, burying redware smooth as calabashes and webbed with black geometric designs to smolder on cedar logs inside a mound of dry sheep dung. Her grandson painted watercolors of *katsinas* in lifelike poses, and I bought a set, which now hangs in my study. That Hopi family's hospitality helped kindle a decades-long affair with the Colorado Plateau and fed an interest in the continent's first people that eventually led me to anthropology and Alaska.

From the rooftop, I see initiates wearing nothing but blankets, who stand with their godparent sponsors, sleep-deprived and hungry from their ordeal. Their near-nakedness signals humility, their bare feet a debt owed to the earth. They spent last night curled fetus-like in the kiva's womb, below a cornmeal line painted on the wall—the path that Maasawu, the Creator, expects them to follow. On the previous day, the *katsinas* had whipped them. When tears flushed their eyes, their godfathers had traded places with them, receiving the blows in their stead. This, too, a promise: if you walk the straight path, Maasawu will take on part of your suffering.

The Mudhead chorus now marches past with its dried-clay masks, heads smooth as urns, eyes and mouths O-shaped, as if in constant surprise. Their big-bellied drum hums in the pit of my stomach. In tune with the fertility theme, clown *katsinas* pretend to hump old women in the crowd. Black ogres chase Hopi tough guys, trying to blacken their faces with soot. Other monsters go from door to door, threatening to eat children who have misbehaved, and demanding fresh meat. Spectators who line the streets pluck feathers from the procession's wake, blessings the *katsinas* left in the dirt. Humor and horseplay mixed with awe and reverence take me by surprise. What I witness reminds me that the sacred and the profane are as much part of a continuum in an eddying universe as the seasons and generations.

Katsinas circle the village four times, always, *always* following the sun's daily and annual course. (We'd call it "clockwise," but abstract time, time detached from the body, has no function in feasts linked to the earth.) The dancers stop on every kiva roof, where the clan priests consecrate them with cornmeal, "feeding" the spirits that have traveled so far. With each round I recognize more characters in the riot of colors and forms.

A Kokopelli Katsina—"a nympho," according to William—sports a woman's kilt and the Hopi woman's sculpted "butterfly" hairdo.

A Mocking Katsina latches onto other *katsinas* and bystanders, mimicking their every move. Dressed in cutoff jeans, modern footwear, hippie pendants, and a beaded vest, he resembles certain White Men.

A Guard Katsina in a checkered kilt points its yucca wand at me. Guards punish any transgression on the *katsinas'* path, and it takes me a few seconds and the example of others on the roof to understand the request to remove my cap.

A Heheya Katsina with a lasso tempts children by holding out woven baskets, *katsina* dolls, bundles of *piki*, or cookies on a string, snaring them when they reach for his gifts. This tempting with riches, and the white-plumed, spruce-ruffed Snow Katsina, bring to mind a controversy that embroils my hometown, Flagstaff, an hour from here as the vulture flies. A ski resort operator plans to use wastewater to supply the barren slopes of the San Francisco Peaks with snow there. Concerned residents, environmental organizations, and Hopi representatives have protested such waste and desecration; but it looks as if the city will go ahead anyhow.

Could the multi-year drought that squeezes the West signal our straying from ground truths, from the straight path? Have we lost sight of priorities in a desert? Dancing for harmony in the world, the Hopi are dancing for all of us.

Toward evening, we drive on to Shongopavi, perched on a spur of Second Mesa. Residents of Old Shongopavi relocated here after the Pueblo uprising of 1680, fearing Apache marauders and reprisals from the Spanish. Outside ideas, diseases, and trappings have taken their toll, but this village remains a stronghold of Hopi tradition. We shiver in sweaters and pile jackets while the supplicants brave the late winter chill bare-chested. There is less levity here, less chasing and teasing. Despite our lighter skin and self-conscious poses, nobody pays us any attention. A different cast of *katsinas* shuffles through Shongopavi's still frozen mud, dwarfed by the wing-helmeted, somber Crow Mother. Yowe, the *katsina* that beheaded the Franciscan priest more than 300 years ago, wields an old saber. Memory runs deep on the mesas, as does the desire for restoration. A few people in the audience ask for canings, to be cleansed and healed. It feels like a foreign place at the heart of America. But no. This *is* the ancient heart of America—wounded but resilient, vibrant, enduring, powered by and powering immemorial cycles.

In a handout for the trip's participants, William had summarized the Hopi worldview. "We must have constant prayer in our hearts, from the minute we are awake till the time we are asleep. We must respect both the spirit and the creation."

"Hopi," William said at one point, "is not a tribe, but a state of being."

At last light, the main kiva swallows the host of *katsinas*. One by one, their feathered silhouettes shrink into the roof hatch. Eventually, only the tip of the ladder that they descended protrudes aboveground, angled at the first stars. The rooftops and streets quickly empty. As we walk back to the dirt parking lot, a TV like a blue eye flickers from a dark house with a satellite dish.

The Last Fifteen Miles

THIS IS A PILGRIMAGE OF SORTS, and like all good pilgrimages, it begins on foot. After the convenience of air-conditioned, motorized travel in a contraption whose model and brand convey status as a trek to Mecca or Jerusalem once did, I set out for the sacred place humbly, in sturdy leather boots.

Trudging through deep red sand, past a gutted mattress and shards of whiskey bottles that glitter like broken dreams, I search for the route into the canyon, down to the Colorado's lobed shores. After avoiding "Lake" Powell and its dam for decades, I finally decided to visit what is left of Glen Canyon. Over the years, I sifted stacks of bleached photos and accounts by travelers lucky enough to have seen the Glen in all its glory. With that historical residue and my knowledge of similar canyons, I've tried to reconstruct loss—a loss felt possibly even deeper because I neither knew the thing lost nor would have a chance to reclaim it. Those from whom it was taken at least have their memories. The damming feels like personal trauma, as there is no other landmark I care to know that has been so completely corrupted while almost staying within reach. I am curious how the place I imagined compares with reality. There is middle-age stocktaking also, which casts its long shadow. I am past fifty now, and the likelihood of seeing the reservoir drained or dried up in my lifetime is slim.

After a tour of the concrete blade that guillotined the river and now marks Mile Zero, the little-used Ropes Trail to the river seemed just the cure for a case of civilization blues. When I had asked about the trailhead's location, a volunteer at the Park Service information desk refused to provide that information, because "it's too dangerous." I guess the agency thinks that rescuing a few cliffed-out, dehydrated hikers or retrieving the bodies of those who, searching for a way down, haplessly missed the edge, is less trouble than facing a liability suit.

I was sure I could find the trail on my own but, apparently, had walked from a hard place into rocks—plenty of them.

Beyond turtleback outcrops, sandstone gives way to sheer space, and, peering over the edge, I cannot see an entrance gully or lower ledge to reach safely. No markers, no cairns. Instead, steel pylons march overland, two-headed robotic grotesques of the mythical Navajo warrior twins. They hum with the river's life force and cables droop from their raised arms into the abyss. On the far rim, the town of Page sprawls across hot sienna flats, still improvised blight, but now catering to golfers and house-boaters rather than dam builders.

Across from town, upstream from where I am scanning the cliffs, the Carl Hayden Visitor Center sticks to Glen Canyon's west rim like a modernist cliff swallow nest. I had opened its mirrored glass doors with trepidation. Would anybody there recognize me as a dissenter, a deserter from the American Dream? Morbid curiosity compelled me to take that guided tour—*know thy enemy!*

Bureau of Reclamation personnel tries hard to keep undesirables from infiltrating the site. Waiting near the desk for the tour to begin, I learned from a cardboard sign that nail clippers and binoculars were among the items forbidden to bring, for security reasons. "Any mentioning of bombs, sabotage, etc., will not be tolerated," the back of my ticket stated. I wondered if a black tapering Visqueen "crack" in the dam face (like the one famously unrolled by Earth First! on the 1981 spring equinox) qualified as sabotage. Plaques mounted below panorama windows vis-à-vis the dam instead bombard visitors with stats, as if the view alone weren't enough. "Height of dam above river level: 583 feet. Maximum thickness at foundation: 350 feet. Generating capacity: 1.3 million kilowatt. Cost: $145,000,000...." The film schedule at the auditorium listed *Desert Oasis*, a cultural and natural history flick about the reservoir, second largest in the United States. In the exhibition area, posters with diagrams and historical photos further trumpeted our species' accomplishments. Strangely, the pageant of progress also included a fish tank in a corner. Boxed-in behind glass, flannelmouth suckers and humpback chubs—streamlined by the turbid Colorado, now endangered by sediment-trapping dams—hung listlessly between neon green plastic plants, suspended in unnaturally clear, filtered water.

Having passed through the airport-style security checkpoint, our motley band stepped into the first elevator and quickly fell to the dam's crest. Our tour guide, Duane, a gray-haired gent with high-riding chinos, probably meant well. Originally from Salt Lake City, he had worked at the Page power plant for thirty years and now enjoyed shepherding tourists for the Glen Canyon Natural History Association. As it turned out, we would not hear much natural history. "Lake Powell gets 2.5 million visitors per year," Duane said with a lisp that at times made him hard to understand. He told us about a dam visitor, who, after Duane had mentioned that in dry years no Colorado River water reaches the Sea of Cortez—a sea that "does not really need it"—commented "Good, we're using it all up."

I wish Duane had taken the time to find out and explain that, before the construction of dams, the Colorado River supplied one of the world's largest desert estuaries. Fed by freshwater and nutrients, these coastal wetlands teemed with beavers, deer, coyotes, numerous species of fish and waterfowl—even jaguars. Farther out, whales, dolphins, and California sea lions cavorted in the fertile mixing of waters. "The river was nowhere and everywhere," Aldo Leopold reminisced about the delta, "for he could not decide which of a hundred green lagoons offered the most pleasant and least speedy path to the Gulf."

We first stopped on the dam crown, at one of the van-size concrete pouring buckets, a memento of construction times. "Five million cubic yards of concrete were poured," Duane boasted, while a uniformed guard loitered nearby. "Cement blocks were cooled with ice water for fourteen days before the next block was set into place." A heavily made-up German woman in a stars-and-stripes vest and straw cowboy hat worried about "ze kracks on ze side of ze dam." Duane assured her that those were the seams of the concrete blocks and perfectly safe. I was more concerned about the lush hanging gardens and tapestry seeps on both canyon walls downstream of the dam. To Duane's credit, he admitted that the reservoir's leakage through porous Navajo sandstone—the dam's anchoring rock—caused those. Fifteen feet lie between Lake Powell's high-water mark and the dam crest; Duane mentioned the 1983 snowmelt, which almost overtopped and threatened the dam and everybody downstream. He also recalled the 5.5 magnitude earthquake of 1993.

Our tour guide moved on to praise the lake's fishing and the annual contests, citing record striped bass that weighed in at forty-eight pounds and eleven ounces. Not a word about the dam's impact on the hard-pressed finned natives downstream, in the Grand Canyon. When I leaned over the parapet on the reservoir side, I spotted an introduced trophy fish near one of the intakes, floating belly-up.

After pausing at the merry-go-round of a display turbine,

we entered a second elevator, bound for the belly of the beast. Bridging the silence in the tight cubicle, Duane informed us that we were passing several inspection galleries on our way down, each equipped with instruments that measure the dam's flex under varying pressure from the reservoir. "It's a living creature," he reminded us. In exiting, I looked up the concrete elevator shaft with slight vertigo. We followed a neon-lit, echoing tunnel chilly as a bunker or meat locker. *More than 100 feet of concrete lie between you and the waters of Lake Powell* read a sign near some drafty hole, and a gray sample polished like gemstones was displayed to be touched. Comforted by its smooth solidity, we emerged on a gallery at the dam's foot. Between the generating station and the dam stretched a buzz-cut, incomprehensibly green lawn—a space level and wide enough for a game of golf—planted, according to Duane, "to make it look nice."

Bulging against the river's might, the blinding, white act of defiance stolidly plugged brick-red canyon walls. At this shrine a society worshipped technology, its own cleverness, but despite the overwhelming gigantism it felt like veneer on the masonry of the ages.

In a way, this concrete atrocity had turned me into a writer. After reading somewhere that 120 canyons flooded as the reservoir level rose, I'd decided some years ago to explore an equal number of canyons on the Colorado Plateau to understand the magnitude of this eradication. Journals I kept during these treks morphed into a bigger story and then into my first book—strange to think that five million cubic yards of congealed hubris have been my muse.

Inside the generating station, from a bridge like that of a ship or a spaceship, we admired a row of eight buttercup-yellow, spinning generators, each the size of a small two-story house and fed by a penstock ("fifteen feet in diameter") that sluiced water down from eight intakes on the reservoir side. An overhead video screen spouted more techno-propaganda, and a sign reminiscent of Soviet-era factories praised *reclamation—108 years of serving the West*. The uneven, hand-drawn *8* showed that the number had been proudly updated every year.

At long last, I spy a black-and-white-banded metal post pounded into slickrock slightly below the rim, in line with several others. Weak-kneed under my heavy pack, I seek traction, shuffling down an exposed sandstone ramp with the posture of a stubborn mule. A chainsaw's nasal drawl rises from the canyon bottom—tamarisk control or firewood for a fisherman's camp? After passing an alcove with cowboy inscriptions, I approach the last and steepest pitch above the river. Here, a steel cable, the trail's eponymous "rope," runs through eyebolts in the wall. Avoiding frayed strands that could draw blood from my palms, I lower myself hand over hand, feet planted firmly against naked rock.

I now have descended roughly the same distance I "traveled" by elevator from the dam's crown to the power plant, but the two trips couldn't be more different.

At the bottom trailhead, the hiker faces a shithouse half as big as some cabins I've lived in. It sits smack-dab in a site of worship, where, thousands of years ago, Desert Archaic hunters chipped elongated, latticed figures with light-bulb heads and "antenna" appendages from the rock varnish. The bullets of imbeciles "killed" the panel's bighorn sheep, the mainstay of people who entrapped spirits in stone, who appeased and bound animals to themselves by magic.

Lightheaded from the heat and the climb, I loll in tamarisk shade, guzzling lukewarm water. Midges whine and a raven talks to its own echo. Below the cliff rim across the river, I notice four test pits for dam sites that engineering geologists considered but ultimately rejected.

I get up and walk upstream to an old cable car, a relic of more optimistic days. The dam that goes with it lies around the bend, out of sight, which is just fine.

Looking for the beach behind the shrubbery belt, I stumble

into a camp like a squirrel's nest, gouged from the tamarisks. Two geezers in folding chairs puff enormous cigars among coolers, solar showers, and fishing paraphernalia. A chainsaw sits on the ground. Looks like they thinned the green canopy to make room for their Bedouin tent.

On the beach's crescent of sand, I unroll my packraft, a five-foot-long, lightweight Hypalon number I had piggybacked to my pack. As I start to inflate it with an ingenious nylon airbag, two motor pontoon boats are pulling up, disgorging gear and kayakers who will paddle downstream, to Lees Ferry. To get a head start and perhaps a camp to myself, I push off right away.

This is my little tub's maiden voyage, and I enjoy its maneuverability (it appears to turn on a dime) and the freedom and ease of travel it affords. Working my shoulder muscles also feels good after the punishing hike. The spark of self-sufficient discovery galvanizes me, as it does after every launch. I stab my twin-bladed paddle into the river, watching water pearl from its edges and momentarily dance on the surface like droplets on a hot stove plate. Little whirlpools follow each stroke, shaped like miniature waterspouts. Fish jump. A cormorant rakes through the afternoon, a stumpy-winged crow. A red-necked grebe dives, leaving haiku pond-ripples. About a quarter mile downstream, a spring splashes from a fern-bearded rock crevice straight into the river, calming as a courtyard fountain. Already, most of the canyon lies wrapped in shadows, but occasionally, low-angle light sheets down a defile, igniting fall-tinged willows and tamarisks on shore. Between sightseeing planes and motorboats that chop into the Glen's tranquility, I can peer through cracks in the present, glimpsing what it must have been like, before. I cannot help but imagine what we would have done regardless, to wring lucre from its allure. Jet tour boats would ply the river as they now do below Moab and above "Lake" Mead. Helicopters would shuttle the rushed rich to and from the canyon. Private permits would be hard to obtain, rock art would be vandalized, riverbanks trampled, campsites overrun.... Yet another quiet place loved to death. Beginning in 1948, Arizona business pioneer Art Greene *did* offer motorized trips from Lees Ferry, upriver to Forbidding Canyon and nearby Rainbow Bridge, spearheading industrial tourism's assault on the Canyon Country. In a way, the Glen seems safer now, ensconced in our memories, our dreams, untouched by crowds or bureaucracy.

At the Honey Draw riffle, the current accelerates; fronds of weed and river cobbles rush by underneath the raft like some Lewis Carroll netherworld as I get sucked onto the glistening tongue. Blowing down the chute, I flinch at licks of icy water.

It is getting late, and I look for a camp. At Ferry Swale, a veritable tent city has mushroomed with lustily burning fires and so I continue. Tamarisks choke the banks, and where they did not find a foothold, erosion has gullied other possible tent sites. Eventually, I make landfall at Mile Nine, near the apex of Horseshoe Bend, where the river doubles back as if to meet with itself.

The canyon's east rim briefly flares like burnished copper before it turns leaden gray. Warm and cool air currents caress me while I fix dinner. Mourning doves mourn what once was. When a breeze combs the tamarisk thickets, the expiring day sighs. Silhouetted walls amplify water shushing across gravel bars, cicadas shrilly pulsing in the bushes, and later, stars shining bright as lit dust motes. Never mind the scattered bottle caps, the hobo hearths of metal-ringed fire pits, or the camp's sign fluorescing in the beam of my headlamp.

I awake to the hollering of some yahoos on the Horseshoe Bend overlook. Sticking my head out of my tent, I see them as ants on the rim, with camera flashlights going off. I briefly consider showing my butt but instead wolf down breakfast, break camp, load up, and go.

The gorge has a Sunday morning feel to it—as a matter of fact, it *is* Sunday. I rest on my elbows, paddle athwart, and yield to the river. Like me, herons inertly survey the scene. In an eddy mallards chuckle as if at some private joke. A raven sculls past, alighting on yet another sign, where he throws back his head and slides some limp thing down his gullet. Twirling on glassy boils, I glide past Finger Rock's pillar, which slips through my field of vision. In some places, blind arches grace the cliffs like walled-off tunnels. Elsewhere, buttresses plunge directly into translucent green depths, leaving no beaches whatsoever.

Across from Waterholes Canyon, fly fishermen enact age-old foraging rituals; casting spider silk from the shallows, they offer time and hope to some wild, pagan river god. Waterholes is one of only two side canyons spared partial or full flooding by the reservoir, one of over a hundred that accounted for Glen Canyon's particular charm. Near Cave Canyon, a skipped piece of slate skims the still surface—a belted kingfisher patrolling for fingerling trout. A peregrine spooks a raft of ducks, which scoot with a sound like a sloughing cutbank. After a failed attempt to bushwhack to Hislop Cave, I watch its black yawn sail past high on river left. Where the cliffs recede, yielding to the more widely eroded Chinle shale and volcanic ash of the Echo Cliffs monocline, an old roadbed to Lees Ferry dips and swerves along the left bank.

Too soon, wall stumps of local stone and the Paria Riffle's unvarying pitch spell the end of Glen Canyon. And thus begins the Grand Canyon, grandest of all, Abbey's "conveyor belt for baloney boats," which I shall leave for some other time, some bigger baloney boat.

Duly impressed and a bit shell-shocked, we had resurfaced in the busy visitor center: The teenage couple holding hands as if on a date. The Euros, always fashionable, seeing the best 'Merica has to offer. The *Jurassic Park* fan getting kicks from nature engineered into amusement. And the dad holding the hand of a four-year-old boy with a bulldozer emblazoned on his T-shirt. As I was preparing to dodge bodies in the lobby and bee-line for the exit, a tall, baldheaded punk turned to me: "Not too bad a tour, huh?"

Not at all. Not at all. Unfortunately, one number had been missing, drowned out by Duane's rote citation, the number of miles between Hite and the dam, the true measure of Glen Canyon before the deluge: 186. It took days, sometimes weeks, to string them together with oar strokes and elbow grease, and each mile was miracle-filled. Only the names survive, evoking mossy grottoes and phallic rocks, ruins, petroglyphs, stone-cut hand-and-toe trails, corkscrew narrows, dripping springs, cottonwood groves, solitude, mystery, history, romance, the poetry of moon-shadow and echoing halls. Twilight Canyon, Tapestry Wall, Klondike Bar, Last Chance Creek, Iceberg Canyon, Cathedral in the Desert, Hole in the Rock, Hidden Passage, Crossing of the Fathers.... I curse the sins of *our* fathers who sacrificed too much beauty for what they mistook for progress. Born too late, I have nothing but these names and the last fifteen miles.

At Home in a Hole in the Rock

I N THE WESTERN GRAND CANYON, when the mercury hits 100 degrees, shade becomes a destination. Water curbs life in this hardscrabble place. Dryness shrinks slickrock pools, condemns tadpoles and fairy shrimps, wicks away sweat. Moving or simply breathing depletes your inner well. If you cannot find water at the end of the day you will have to backtrack to it on the next.

Halfway down the layer cake of the ages, I walk on the pumpkin-colored, level Supai Group, feasting my eyes on the scenery. As summer radiation parboils my neck and pack straps dig into my shoulders, I scan the sandstone benches for refuge. Below, on a natural patio next to an outcrop, an old horseshoe snags my attention. I drop the pack to scout and discover an opening, stone gaping like a whale's jaws.

This alcove housed people once. Its centerpiece, rodent-ravaged bedding, is folded neatly and weighted with a rock. It looks as if the most recent cave dweller stepped out to attend to his horse and never came back. There is firewood, a Dutch oven, a torn bag spilling flour, a can of lard and another of Calumet

45

(the baking powder with the hatchet-nosed chief)—it could have been biscuit or pancake day. There's a tin of Prince Albert tobacco, sporting His Highness, frocked and ramrod-straight. There is coffee of course, and a coffeepot, a glass jar of pitch or molasses, a box of matches that look like they would still light, a double-blade ax, and blackened silverware. Against the wall, two wooden panniers for hauling all this stuff sit beneath a rough-scratched date: 1942.

I picture the lone buckaroo dodging summer's inferno while another, manmade hell raged in the South Pacific. Clearly, he had meant to return.

Brick-red marks smudge the back wall, which flakes with age. On closer inspection I notice centipede-like designs that hunter-gatherers painted eons ago. The same need pulled us all here—nomads, sun-blasted, sore, looking for rest, snug in Earth's pocket.

I've escaped to this back of beyond from yammering neighborhood dogs, from the din of Route 66, from my town's narrowness and barbed opinions. When I left there, the peaks had gone from green to gray, and the industrial outskirts seemed even bleaker than usual. My two-week retreat into the Grand Canyon thus also marks a last hurrah in the sun before I crawl into winter's deep cave.

The ground outside—the same slickrock that roofs the alcove—is smooth terracotta, intermittently pitted and cracked. The region is infamous for its lack of water, except during the monsoons, when potholes form a lifeline of fleeting reservoirs. Routes here do not lose or gain much elevation but by skirting each side canyon, add miles to distance as the vulture flies. Progress through this terrain is always painful and seldom straightforward. Limestone chunks from the layers above the Supai abrade hiking boots and shins. Catclaw, bear grass, brush, and agaves lacerate skin. June can roast marrow, January freeze a brain.

Permian winds laid this pavement, grain by crystalline grain. The fossilized dunes cap a terrace 200 yards to a mile wide, known as the Esplanade. Two thousand feet above the Colorado River and roughly the same distance below the canyon's North Rim, it winds drunkenly around nooks, springs, and peninsulas from Crazy Jug Canyon to the Toroweap viewpoint and beyond. At points in-between, the Esplanade juts into space in balconies above silent depths. Every once in a while, when the air does not stir, the whispering of rapids reaches an overlook.

Water that gnaws at sedimentary rock carves out hollows that, in size and acoustics, can range from cubbyhole to concert hall. At Mesa Verde in Colorado and near Arizona's Navajo Mountain, vast alcoves harbor entire settlements: tiered citadels, apartment hives, towers, and plazas that buzzed at the same time Europe was building cathedrals. The Grand Canyon's alcoves are smaller and less widely known, but the spark of discovery keeps me coming back here. In theory, on all public lands, federal laws protect cultural relics more than fifty years old, be they cowboy paraphernalia or Indian rock art. Pothunters and vandals, however, blight the land, and I'm always surprised to see such treasures in place, undisturbed.

With soot on the ceilings, dust tracked by generations of mice, and rusty-tin middens nearby, the Esplanade's abodes differ drastically from the romanticized chuck wagon camps of John Ford Westerns. Spend a few hours in one and you'll taste not campfire wistfulness but hardship and hardheadedness, the hermit's self-imposed exile and deprivation. Dents in a washbasin. An ax handle mended with wire. A hoof with a horseshoe attached, and leg bones, like an oracular throw of the dice. One room-size shelter holds the headgear of a bighorn, full curls chipped in duels, tips rubbed to stubs, "broomed" when they interfered with the ram's vision, the skull plate nibbled by calcium-starved rodents. Did he die of sickness, injury, or old age, comforted by the shade? Did a mountain lion drag him in, feasting concealed? Did a hunter 800 years ago honor his life there, or perhaps all life, with some private ritual? I can find no bones close by to untangle the riddle.

In this stark landscape alcoves anchor not just the body but also the mind. Bedded down on slickrock under star-strewn infinity, far from rainfall or rescue but near the abyss, even the hardiest soul feels a shiver. Cradled by stone instead, you ignore what could keep you awake.

A seep above the Supai, which a stockman with a dynamite stick had supposedly tried to enhance and which I hoped to tap, turns out to be barren. Luckily, as the rim's shadows flood the patio, bringing chills in their wake, I find a gallon of rank effluent a stone's throw from the alcove, where runoff has guttered the bedrock. This must be part of the shelter's appeal: the only water for miles around.

About a week into my trip I haven't seen anybody. I enter a fissure that starts in the Esplanade and entrenches deeper and deeper toward Kanab Creek. The largest Grand Canyon tributary on the north side and one of few major water sources in the Arizona Strip, Kanab Creek runs only sporadically. It feeds redbuds and single-leaf ash, and it beads hanging gardens of flowers and maidenhair fern, a fine break from drab blackbrush and cactus fields. I plan to follow the creek for a while before exiting its canyon and climbing back to the Esplanade. I long for its soothing touch, which will cool my scrapes and rinse the dust off my body. Only last spring I camped under the cottonwoods on its banks, lulled by the water's soliloquy.

Where the tributary widens into Kanab Canyon, I do a double take and again check my map. But I haven't made a mistake—the creek has been silenced, its bed choked with dust. Mud like unfired clay splinters underfoot. Cobblestones crunch where the current once slid across gravel bars. I'm in shock. Is this the result of drought or of siphoning for irrigation by ranches in the creek's upper parts?

There is a third possible culprit, I realize as I trudge between thickets: tamarisk, the scabrous pest that bleeds the Southwest. The lacy-leafed growth crowds out native willows and cottonwoods, concentrates salt in the soil, and sinks taproots that lower the groundwater table.

After an hour or so, I arrive at a pool ringed with mud that checks my progress in the creek bed. An agave tip long ago punctured and drained my plastic water jug, and the bladder in my backpack has only a pint left. But the dregs of this stream in retreat are too thick to be filtered into drinking water. Disappointed and dehydrated, I bushwhack around the gunk hole and push on.

Toward noon, eager to leave this husk of a waterway, I nose up a side canyon that could lead to the Esplanade. One of its forks soon ends in a sandstone balcony three stories above. A second fork beckons like a mirage: sinuous, wavering, promising. Sculpted walls block the sun's stare, and, smooth as a sidewalk, the bottom holds lenses of clear water. I fall to my knees and kiss one greedily, not bothering with filter or cup.

I round what I hope will be the last bend before the drainage tops out but am stopped by a rock fall. Cabin-size boulders lie on edge, stacked into a lethal gym, a disaster zone riddled with crawl spaces. A possible route through this mess starts with stemming between two angled monoliths. I place one foot and both hands before pushing up and into the crack in one quick move.

The sickening crunch of pulled gristle registers an instant before the pain in my right shoulder does.

I slide back to the ground. Something is seriously wrong. The limb feels useless, not part of me. I am suddenly lightheaded, which masks the black ache. This is the fourth time I've dislocated this shoulder, though never before so far from help. By now I know the drill. Let your arm dangle, muscles relaxed. Rotate your upper body, carefully, back and forth. Avoid any grinding of bone on bone. When the humerus head and the torso's socket align just so, the limb will slip into its joint, smooth as a chambered bullet.

And it does, after several tries.

This is no country for men past their prime, or for the lame. This is why the Park Service had me sign a liability waiver, warning against an "unusually difficult and potentially dangerous" hike.

With my arm pressed to my rib cage, hand tucked into my waistband for support, I scramble back down the canyon. At the first of the water pockets, I make camp on the slickrock. Fixing dinner more or less one-handed, I feel like a bird with a clipped wing. Where the geology offers shelter, as it does on the Esplanade, I travel without a tent. Tonight, with cold stars throbbing overhead, I wish for a hole to curl up in and lick my wounds.

Days later, back on the Supai highway, stiff-shouldered but still making miles, I come upon Bean Cave, whose former lodger I've read about. A signature at eye level in the shallow niche claims it as one of Walapai Johnnie's far-flung dens. In 1928, young John D. "Walapai Johnnie" Nelson joined the search for river runners Glen and Bessie Hyde, who'd vanished on their honeymoon voyage through the Grand Canyon. Johnnie had fought in the Philippines and later worked as a pack-trip guide around these parts. Often blind drunk by noon, he was nevertheless popular with the outfitters who fired and rehired him, according to one boss, about fifty times every season. A 1954 Kodak ad shows him herding dudes past Bryce Canyon hoodoos. Smiling, he leans on his paint pony, relaxed in batwing chaps, hat tipped back rakishly. You can tell he was charming, a spinner of yarns, fully at ease, someone you'd want as a guide—a spitting image of my younger, wrangling-days self, I'd like to think, except for his raven hair. He must have had grit. He built the trail that drops precipitously through the Supai to a leaf-shaded spring named after him. By the time I've panted back up from there to the Bean Cave, my water bottles are almost empty again.

The vestiges of Walapai Johnnie's tenure in the Grand Canyon transport me back to my own days of working on horseback. My alcove then was a twelve-foot, oven-like trailer near Tucson that contained a two-burner gas stove, legions of flies, and pints of sand, sifted in through the cracks. I was living my Western dream, guiding for a trail-riding outfit in the Santa Catalina Mountains. Broke, exhausted, and reeking of stables, I cut short my cowboy "career" when some nag kicked my chest and I had to pay for x-rays myself.

Before I set out on the last leg of my journey—Johnnie's former commute, a century-old switchback that could kill a mule—I meet three backpackers fresh from the North Rim. Perched on a boulder, legs primly crossed, I chat for a while with their young female leader. As they get up to leave, I stand and pivot, facing the group to hide my half-bare behind. After weeks of abuse from sandpaper rocks, my lone pair of shorts hangs in tatters. I'm wearing a T-shirt, boots, a crooked smile, and not much else. I must look like the hobo king of the alcove clan. I probably smell like him too.

Classroom with a View

P ARKER, LOOKING A BIT LIKE a young Al Pacino, gasps as he steps waist-deep into the "warmer" shallows of the reservoir-fed Colorado River near the Grand Canyon's Cathedral Wash. Together with trip leader and river guide Sarah, he walks a seine net on poles through backwaters muddied by the Paria River's sediment, which has dyed the normally bottle-green stream below Lees Ferry milk-coffee brown. The first sweep of this preferred habitat of juvenile fish yields one polka-dotted rainbow trout fingerling and two native speckled dace. Beginning in the 1920s, the National Park Service introduced rainbow and brown trout into Grand Canyon tributaries like Bright Angel Creek, for the pleasure of sport fishermen. After the completion of Glen Canyon Dam, the now clear and frigid waters that jet from its spillways were stocked with more trout. These trout in the river's main stem have become a threat to the canyon's native fish species—humpback chubs, flannelmouth, and bluehead suckers; they compete for food and prey on the young of these rare or endangered species.

As one of ten teenagers, Parker embarked on a weeklong adventure with Grand Canyon Youth (GCY), a nonprofit utilizing this concourse of light as one of the world's most exciting classrooms. The Flagstaff-based program promotes stewardship for public lands and learning through participation in all aspects of a trip. Five guides, a student coordinator, and a United States Geological Survey scientist act as mentors as well as instructors on this one.

To get a grip on the science and routines of a river journey, the youths are assigned to groups with daily rotating tasks: cook crew, dishes crew, toilet or "groover" crew, and science crew. Every evening, the science crew sets baited and non-baited fish traps—treble hoop nets with different mesh sizes—from the beaches at camp. One type of bait, the artificial "stinky cheese" for catfish, soon gains notoriety among the students.

The different setups serve to determine the most effective method for removing nonnative fish. Past attempts by the Park Service to weed out the unwanted have largely failed. Electro-shocking stuns fish, which then float to the surface where the "aliens" can be gathered, but it can also injure the rare or endangered ones.

After running a warm-up rapid at Badger Creek, the students are busy preparing lunch sandwiches under leaden clouds that bloom in typical monsoon-season style. A lashing rain shower briefly checks the three-digit temperature. Drifting downstream in the rafts, the guides get acquainted with students whose interests and personalities quickly emerge. The motivations for coming on a trip are as diverse as the GCY students' backgrounds. Matthew, tall, blond, and politically savvy, once stood on the South Rim during a geology school project and decided to hike to the river or float it some day. Joshua, part Hopi and the son of a former Grand Canyon outfitter, has wanted to visit some of the canyon's powerful places since age fourteen. "Aly," a South Korean fireplug, joined court-ordered, on probation but also likes private river trips.

Many first-timers get hooked on river life and keep coming back for more, validating GCY's mission: to inspire curiosity about a landscape and its natural communities. The Flagstaff program director sees students as fires to be kindled rather than vessels to be filled, though we do need to keep them hydrated. Assisting the USGS and NPS with their research introduces them not only to methods of aquatic biology and stream ecology, but also to the ways different land-management agencies operate. Some might even pick a career, among cacti, scorpions, and snakes.

Long before they launched at Lees Ferry, these teenagers performed community service, two hours for each day they'll spend on the river. They volunteered in Flagstaff's soup kitchen, at orphanages in Peru, or with the Arizona Desert Bighorn Sheep Society, building rainwater catchment basins. Sara, a GCY alumna with a nose stud and thumb rings repaired houses in post-Katrina New Orleans. "GCY definitely got me started on the idea of service," she says, self-assured. On this trip, she takes turns at the oars and ends up rowing Grapevine, a bouncy 8 on the Grand Canyon's 1 to 10 scale of whitewater. A pre-med student interested in working for Doctors Without Borders, Sara seeks to reconcile social and environmental activism. She is so smitten with GCY that she considers working summers at the warehouse or, one of her dreams, rowing a baggage raft.

Students like Sara, or Parker, or Parker's twin brother Cody, who could be surfing his home beaches near Malibu instead of spending much of his summer on a working-and-learning vacation, seem like another endangered species. Their appetite for natural science and outdoor activities cannot be taken for granted. Visits to U.S. national parks steadily increased from the 1930s until 1987. Since then, backcountry use of these parks has been declining by a little more than one percent each year, possibly as the result of a more sedentary lifestyle. Youngsters in particular seem to suffer from "nature deficit disorder," a term coined by Richard Louv, author of *Last Child in the Woods*.

Louv links the absence of nature in children's lives largely to our obsession with television, video games, the Internet, and iPods. He sees rising rates of obesity, attention disorders, and depression as consequences of this break between the young and nature. Declining knowledge of our national parks eventually might lead to a society that is less concerned with conservation. The preeminent threat to places like the Grand Canyon, even more serious than extinctions, is that future generations could lose touch with them or will consider them mere playgrounds.

Another danger to the canyon becomes explicit to the participants of this trip. Since 1996, Glen Canyon Dam has released three controlled peak floods to improve fish habitat by mimicking pre-dam conditions. Floods inundate the river's dry side channels and depressions, forming backwaters in which juvenile chubs and other native fish hatch and hang out. The water is slightly warmer in these natural hatcheries, and the young fish are protected from strong currents. Experimental releases from the sediment-trapping dam also replenish eroding beaches— habitat for numerous plant and animal species and the location of archaeological sites in the river corridor. Ideally, such releases are timed to coincide with the rains that flood tributaries like the Paria, whose sediment load they deposit throughout the main canyon. To help fine-tune the dam's discharge, Adopt-a-Beach, an ongoing service project by the Park Service, enlists river runners to monitor the canyon's beaches, documenting changes through repeat photography. Replicating the angles of photos taken after the last artificial flood in 2008, the students who scramble across baking boulders quickly understand that North Canyon's shoreline qualifies as a success. We snap a group photo on the restored beach and shove off, but only after a many-voiced, unselfconscious shout of GCY's slogan: "Yay, Science!"

At camp we gather each night for student presentations, which can range from knot tying, or the medicinal properties of Mormon tea, to the landscape painter Thomas Moran.

Tonight, Matthew talks about flashfloods and drives home his points with a water-filled bucket and a wet-sand model of a deathtrap canyon.

But not everything is serious science; our itinerary leaves ample time for play and contemplation, both of which help to create a relaxed learning environment. As an antidote to the stifling heat, our mob douses two baby-blue motor pontoon boats—Behemoths compared to our rafts—only to find that our bailing buckets are no match for the long-range squirt guns of their passengers.

At Redwall Cavern, which gapes in the cliffs like the mouth of a whale shark and which could seat hundreds, a game of Ultimate Frisbee leaves the mud-daubed youths panting and a dust cloud hovering in the air. While we take in the view from the cavern's back, a moment of silence settles over the group. We stand still and listen to a riffle murmuring in the sunlight outside.

There obviously is a physical dimension to learning. Laboring to the top of the Redwall at Eminence Break, Matthew pauses on the trail. "Phew! I've got even more respect now for the ancient Puebloans," he says, wiping his brow with a bandana. The fault line at Eminence Break marks a cross-canyon route to the North Rim by way of the Anasazi footbridge, whose remains we saw from the river, wedged into a chimney up high. Some students peel and sample *tunas*, the wine-dark fruits of the prickly pear that were an ingredient in the ancients' diet. On calm water stretches, they row rafts. One will take over the boatman's seat when his guide is washed out in a rollercoaster rapid. A few will swim rapids, voluntarily and involuntarily, learning when to breathe (in a wave trough) and when not to breathe (counterintuitively, on a wave's crest).

Creature comforts and inconvenience are equally part of this educational package. At President Harding camp, students bathe in the eddy, and Sara takes scissors to Matt's mop head—a strangely domestic scene. Just after dinner, we notice a haze near the South Rim. The light turns cadaverous, the air brisk above the dulled river. A few minutes later, a wind gust whips spray from the water, headed straight for our beach. When it hits, a gigantic dust devil ravages camp. Folding tables get flattened; ground sheets, clothing, and tarps take off on the gyrating column. Students escape the pelting into the bow of the raft I've been captaining, where, hardly sheltered but comfy, they tell worst-injury stories until the wind dies down and a gibbous moon paints Tatahatso Point ghostly white.

With the daily setting and retrieving of nets and the smell of stinky-cheese bait wafting through camp, our conversations inevitably return to the subject of fish, specifically the humpback chub. The pre-dam Colorado's seasonally varying water temperature, suspended sediment, and flow shaped the fish with the telltale submarine bulge. We learn from Parker's student presentation that the federally endangered chub rarely thrives outside the Grand Canyon anymore; only six populations remain in the wild. The largest of these, numbering fewer than 10,000 individuals, now lives and spawns near the mouth of the Little Colorado.

Government scientists routinely catch and tag chubs to assess their habits and numbers. Beginning in 2009, they helicoptered young humpback chubs to Shinumo Creek forty-five miles downstream, to establish another viable population and thereby hedge bets against the species' extinction through any localized, catastrophic event. Highway 89 crosses the Little Colorado at Cameron, and a tanker truck wreck could easily wipe out the colony at the confluence.

Not too surprisingly, when the science crew pulls the fish traps at a camp near there, three humpback chubs flop in the nets. Passing them through a hoop scanner, the students realize that two of the fish already carry micro-transmitter identity tags. Handling the fish as they would kittens, they measure total body length and the length of the forked tail, which indicate age—but the untagged specimen does not want to be measured. In a spastic reflex, it leaps off the measuring board, jackknifing toward the river's edge in an effort to escape. A student grasps it and gently puts it in a bucket, rinsing the sand from its gills and opalescent skin. After they have finished recording the capture data, Sarah injects a chip the size of a rice grain into cartilage of the fish's belly with a sterilized syringe. The students then place the captives back in the river, where they resume their aquatic pursuits.

In the parade of days that constitutes river time, the students have reached the end of their journey. Tomorrow, before sunrise, they will climb out of Pipe Creek, following the Bright Angel Trail to the South Rim. Another group and their coordinator will hike in to the lower Grand Canyon, for their eight-day float through the planet's past.

As dusk drains all color from Cremation camp, the gang circles up around a sacred datura plant to watch one of its moon-flowers unfurl for the nocturnal affair with the sphinx moth, its pollinator. Tanned and a bit disheveled, the students let the trip pass in review. "Until now, I've never had an interest in geology," says Hayden. Matthew enjoyed getting to know people from different backgrounds. "You don't have to have electronics to have fun," admits Matt, who taxed the guides' patience with his short attention span. Parker is surprised how pristine the inner canyon felt, despite thousands of visitors per year. Asked what they will miss most, one of them thinks the sound of the river. Asked how this trip might affect their future, another thinks he'll be more mindful, trying to live with the earth, instead of against it. Some GCY alumni veer more concretely into new directions. Motivated by their Grand Canyon experience, former students have begun to study geology, fisheries biology, or environmental policy. Rennie, from our lower-half trip, wants to become a stream ecologist like her dad. Paul, whose student presentation focused on knot tying, intends to go into engineering to develop outdoor equipment for people with special needs after traveling with that population on two GCY River Buddies trips.

Our journey below the rim has loosed something inside a few of these youths, something like rockfall, the course of which, though inevitable, can never be safely predicted. But regardless of the path they will choose, regardless of whether or not they will speak out in defense of wild places, I daresay that none will forget the days spent among red cliffs and thundering rapids in the company of strangers, some of whom became friends.

Confessions of a Cat Lover

> I do not know much about gods; but I think that the river
> Is a strong brown god—sullen, untamed and intractable...
>
> —T. S. ELIOT, *The Dry Salvages* (1941)

THE STRUCTURE PUT-PUTTING down the Colorado River below Moab resembles a Klingon mother ship. Or perhaps the microscopic view of some weird protein: six H-shaped molecules grouped around an elliptical one. The molecules are lashed to a motor-powered support raft. Bold letters on the tubes proudly announce this traveling circus: Outward Bound.

This is a private trip, an "invitational" solely consisting of Utah instructors who work for this well-respected outdoor education program. These people were *not* sent by their parents. They are here because they are fearless women and men. Almost all of them have as many river miles under their bow as wrinkles on their faces. But there are a few rookies along, as well as logistics staff who keep the Moab program base stocked with boxes of hardtack (the infamous "plate armor"), dehydrated onion soup, bloat-inducing summer sausage, two different kinds of flavorless cheese, and bottles of Pepto-Bismol. Most of the figures on board recline to the stuttering of gangsta music with counter-beat coughs from a four-stroke with a mind of its own. Only one man, the program director, stands proud and alert, at the helm. Occasionally, he tilts the motor and lifts the propeller to avoid plowing sandbanks or gravel bars, which in a low-water year seem to make up the bulk of the river. The raft's repair kit holds a spare propeller, just in case.

They are on a three-day trip in November through Cataract Canyon after a long and rewarding summer season. A mere three-day trip through "Cat," as river rats call it affectionately, is an unforgivable sin. But that is all the time they have before they move on to more gainful unemployment, on the ski slopes of Colorado.

Their run through Cat is a first, a piece of history in the making. They are test pilots all, about to take on formidable whitewater, on crafts with a reputation for being "capricious." The boaters call them "paddle cats," or sometimes "pieces of feces." It needs to be seen if they could safely carry students through these rapids.

What exactly does a paddle cat look like? Imagine a medieval apparatus of torture strapped to a set of inflatable tubes. Two seats resembling the rock-hard benches of workout machines ride atop linked twin pontoons. They are integrated with aluminum foot guards and front bars under which the pilot may wedge his or her knees for leverage and balance. Between the tubes sags a drop hatch of very limited storage capacity. In it, watermelons, signal flares, Band-Aids, instructor manuals, driftwood for campfires, a drybag with costumes, or other essentials may be carried. Seated paddlers are easily mistaken for Easy Riders of the waves, or for monkeys straddling monstrous rubber bananas.

The frame of this Procrustes chair has been designed specifically for our program. No expenses were spared. Rumor has it that a miniaturized prototype was tested in the program director's bathtub, with a blow dryer operated by his girlfriend simulating strong headwinds. The laudable idea behind the design was that student pairs would have to communicate and cooperate to maneuver this...boat.

That is the theory. But it does not matter much yet, on this overcast late-autumn day. Right now, bags of peanut butter-filled pretzels are ripped, and the crew contentedly chews their cud.

Soon enough, we beach our unwieldy landing craft near a camp known as Tamarisk Hell. The scene that unfolds is reminiscent of the Omaha sector on D-Day. Instructors leap into the shallows. (At this time of year they make it to shore without being strafed by mosquitos.) They unload crates of food, stoves, pails, sleeping bags, gas cartouches, the boombox, and Frisbee missiles, camp chairs, Therm-A-Rests, jerry cans of drinking water, a grill, and a fire pan; they clip life jackets, uncoil ropes, and wrestle with tarps or tents. Someone in a rush finds a room with a view for the "Thunderjug," a portable toilet required by Park Service regulations. One also may hear the troops refer to the receptacle coyly as "The Unit." This device evolved from a primitive ancestor. Its Ur-form was "The Groover," an army-issued steel box for grenade launchers, bearing a stenciled warning: CAUTION—EXPLOSIVES! Before the era of cushioned toilet seats, lengthy sessions on this rocket box caused additional indentations in bare backsides—hence the name.

The evening is spent pleasantly enough, over tall tales and burritos, washed down with liberal amounts of mood-enhancing beverages.

Next morning, the time has come to face harsh realities. The mother ship is broken up, and instructor pairs launch their cats. My copilot is Heather. Heather is half my age, twice as graceful, and works three times as hard at the Moab base. Her doe-brown eyes brim with an unspoken question: you know what you're doing, right? While I ready the boat, I try hard to avoid her gaze.

Our rig immediately displays typical cat behavior: it turns as if on a swivel, but the tracking sucks. I try my best to keep its nose pointed downstream. Unlike on an oar-powered double-tube cataraft with a single boatman ideally in control, it is much harder to synchronize the paddle strokes of two people—especially when nobody wants to be captain. As a result, we zigzag down the still-placid river like a drunken water strider.

My mind turns to Outward Bound courses where I've worked with these craft. A favorite pastime of students on calm stretches is "flatwater polo." Two mobs of kayakers attempt to toss a water bottle between the tubes of a paddle cat, while the seated "goalies" are defending that space viciously with their paddles. (We always make them wear helmets for this.) It's a free-for-all, without rules whatsoever. Tackling, biting, splashing, ramming, flipping, and dunking opponents, slinging mud or holding them back by their stern loops—anything goes.

Some cynics maintain that this is the only use for a P-Cat.

One time on the San Juan, after fierce winds kicked the river into frenzy and formed an invisible wall, everybody had to deboard. With throw-bag ropes clipped to the frames, we waded the river, dragging cats downstream and to camp. Except when we stepped into holes in the river bottom, momentarily disappearing. A few kayakers harnessed their boats in front of the deadweights, pulling them like building blocks for Egyptian pyramids. Another low-water year, that one.

Before I even get to have my first muscle spasm, the rumbling of Brown Betty, our first rapid, jolts me from fond memories. The river is flush with sediment from recent rainfalls upstream, and right now its eponymous convulsion resembles a Bloody Mary more than anything else. Those old backpacker knees hurt like hell, so I don't bother folding my six-foot frame into the contraption. I am sure I can ride this baby like a rocking chair.

Due to slight communication problems, we enter the rapid sideways. Next thing, I look up at the raft, catching Heather's expression, that age-old *Why are you leaving me at a time like this?* Her face could use some rouge right now. "What do I do?" she yells over the din. "Try to keep the damn thing—" I swallow the rest of my answer with a pint-size gulp of sludgy Colorado. At this point, I seriously consider finishing this trip in the water, safe and snug in my life jacket. But solidarity gets the better of me, and with the help of my maiden in brilliant neoprene I remount the cat. No need to mention that I did not dress for a swim. I begin to shiver instantly, and my teeth chatter so hard I worry about breaking a filling.

On a previous trip I was lucky to retrieve a half-full pint bottle of Jim Beam doing rounds in an eddy. It probably washed out of a boat flipped by one of the munching holes for which this canyon is known. In my present state, some of that Southern anti-freeze would sure come in handy.

Perhaps it would even improve my aim. Sober, I miss the fun of the standing monster wave at Rapid #10 by overcompensating for the current pushing outward at the bend. The half-moon of fine-grained sand directly below promises heaven: the canyon's best beach camp. Everybody else who lands looks as dry and unconcerned as the surrounding desert.

Tonight's entertainment consists of various party tricks, including pouring blue flames from a bottle, and walking around with bottle caps in your eye sockets and belly button without dropping them. The starred attraction is a bacon-grease bomb in the campfire, which leaves everybody in awe and the performer with singed eyebrows. A proposal to run an obstacle course with quarters pinched between butt cheeks, to be dropped into a bucket at the finish, finds only little resonance with the crowd. Most of us retire early, satisfied by an honest day's work and a steep learning curve.

On our last day, a challenging trio of big drops awaits us, bellowing downstream. The lump in my stomach may not entirely be the result of overdosing on a breakfast of syrup-drenched pancakes, eggs, and cowboy coffee. ("It ain't cowboy coffee if it doesn't dissolve a spoon or float a horseshoe.")

Rapid #15 is merely a warm-up. Early river runners on a mining expedition christened this roller coaster in 1891. Their version of Kilroy-Was-Here, scratched on a boulder on shore, cheerfully reads: *camp # 7, hell to pay, no. 1 sunk & down.* "Number One" was half of their miserable fleet of wooden tubs. A purported ledge of pure silver in the Grand Canyon they were chasing turned out to be nothing but mica and schist, fools' dreams glittering in the sun.

Four notorious marker rocks spiking this stretch of river line up like a baseball diamond. Perhaps the fact that I grew up playing soccer affects the nature of our run. While we are scraping first base the old Abbot and Costello routine flashes through my head. I don't know who or what is on first, but without the cat's foot guard, my toes and kneecap would be. This feels more like pinball than baseball.

"Left turn." "Not so much—I mean, *right* turn!" "Stop!" "Back—paddle!"

We barely miss the pitcher's mound, and a merciful current carries us clear of second base. Not exactly a home run, but we are alive.

While my brain soaks in a marinade of adrenalin, memories of a past near-disasters rear their ugly heads. Only a few weeks before, one of the rafts on an Outward Bound course had smashed sideways into first base. The metal pin of one oarlock broke, and the oar itself bent like putty. But improvisation is a leitmotif in every river runner's life, a talent equally well applied to dressing, cooking, finances, car maintenance, and courtship, sometimes with unorthodox results. With a dexterity acquired over decades in the Great Outdoors and somebody else's penknife, I had sawed a length from bleached bones of driftwood that littered our beach. I whittled it down to the diameter of the fractured pin. I rammed it into the oarlock, thrilled by my own cunning, and then slid in a spare oar. We pushed off into the current. After a few strokes my homemade splint shattered under the strain. Climbing back onto my seat from the bottom of the raft, I felt consoled that, at least, they didn't chain us to the benches anymore. Not easily defied by the river's verdict, we replaced the useless joint with three buff paddlers on starboard. Under the scrutiny of other outfits our lopsided act negotiated the rest of the rapids with the grace of a crippled crab. The guides of the competition hooted and catcalled from recliners on shore, toasting our effort with cans of cold beer. Beneath life jackets adorned with graffiti and the company logo, our chests inflated with pride. Not only had we saved face as individual boatmen once more, but we also upheld the reputation of our fine outdoor program.

At Big Drop One, our only job is to keep her straight and not get bucked off. If I wore a hat, this is the part where I would slap my thighs with it, whooping and hollering. I feel like a centaur, half man, half rubber duck.

Our run through Big Drop Two is so-so, but at least uneventful. Idyllic Little Niagara rushes by, too fast to allow us to make a mistake. The cat in front of us is less fortunate: it parks on a tabletop boulder, tubes half out of the water. The pilots shift their weight, trying to wriggle her off—in vain. Eventually the captain steps out onto the boulder. She puts some muscle to it, straining until I'm afraid her head might burst. When there is sudden movement, she almost misses the boat.

Then comes the big one of the Big Ones. Naturally, we miss the boulder gate of the entrance slot, running a pour-over this side of Mossy Rock instead. We spear almost vertically into the accompanying hole, leaning back in our seats like choreographed bull riders. In an out-of-body experience, I observe the peculiar response of the cat as it bobs back out with a corklike move. Before I have a chance to thumb my nose at Satan's Gut, we have been flushed out at the tail of the rapid.

By now, my copilot has even stopped cursing me under her breath.

The worst lies behind us, or so we think. A rambunctious wind starts to blow, crimping the water's surface. It shoulders the cats into a wide eddy, where they sit like decoy ducks. When I look to shore, the scenery still floats by but in the wrong direction. The baggage boat manned by our junior instructor Mikey seems to fare slightly better, with its twelve-foot-long oars.

Eternities of paddle strokes and teeth gnashing later, I see the mouth of Gypsum Canyon cleave sandstone parapets on river left. The four-day hike to the highway should feel like a Club Med vacation. I am glad I announced my intention to leave our party here, *before* the trip. Let nobody blame my Momma for raising a quitter.

I soon stand on shore, trying to straighten from my Neanderthal posture. Looking at boiling clouds the color of slate, I wonder what further boating adventures I shall miss. With a sigh of relief and a strange popping from my knee, I hoist my sixty-pound pack and wave the disappearing flotilla goodbye.

Vermilion Light

W HAT ATTRACTS US TO NEW PLACES? What compels us to stuff our car trunk or backpack, to once again brave marathon drives, truck-stop fare, or the Byzantine requirements of land managers for a backcountry permit? The trigger can be an aside by a friend. A snippet of history stumbled upon. A rumor of rock art or refuge. Or simply a name.

As first snow dusts the ashen peaks that front my hometown and the sun's arc flattens, Arizona's Vermilion Cliffs promise light glorious and exuberant, a last taste of summer. In these waning days of the year, I long for the palette of canyon light, for pastels refracted by sandstone facades, for arches and alcoves, towers and buttresses varnished and richly aglow.

Fall is my favorite time in the canyons. The mosquitoes and deerflies are gone, and so are most tourists. Clear, tranquil days succeed each other gleaming like childhood memories. Beneath vegetal decay, I sense a sweet feeling of loss in the air, which pinches the heart. Gold briefly ennobles box elders and cottonwoods before winter's rude disrobing.

The hardest part of each morning is stepping into the icy stream, soaking my socks and boots. Knee-deep in the Paria, I resign myself to numb feet and a sunburned neck before reaching camp in the afternoon, where a cup of joe will take off the edge. Aside from the water and air temperature, in the upper canyon the season's advanced stage is not obvious. Growth is sparse here at all times—rabbitbrush, coyote willow, and tamarisk cling to shallow soil pockets. The odd box elder has not yet shed its serrated leaves or even changed color. Pillars and crosshatched whalebacks rise above the still canyon rims, sentinels from the past watching over the present.

Upstream of the famous narrows, waves of Page sandstone and the red Carmel formation abut the wash with swirled ice-cream flavors. Strawberry. Butterscotch. Pumpkin. Vanilla. The variegated rock chronicles floods that alternated over millions of years between muddy, tinted and sandy, clear. More recent runoff has sculpted eccentricities from this matrix, hourglasses and Swiss-cheese textures, cracks, niches, and lattices, and pockets filled with smooth-pebble gifts—perfect hideouts for lizards or gnomes.

Backpacking was my first outdoor love and, despite the forced marches of army days, remains my preferred mode of travel. It provides a sense of self-sufficiency and independence I rarely experience in a world hedged with constraints and demands. As a snail carries its shell, I carry all essentials—food, shelter, and extra clothes—humbly on my back. Except for spiritual nourishment and the miracles of chance encounters I expect nothing but water from this place. (Ecstasy is always welcome, a bonus.) My pack even has room for some luxuries: a folding chair, a pint of Scotch, flip flops for camp, *War and Peace*. I never read about the desert while I venture there, afraid that another writer's view could become mine. The plight of the *Grande Armée* in Russia's snowy wastes keeps me cool and by contrast, comforted. It is good to remember: ordeals could be so much worse.

True, each additional pound is paid for with sweat; but the longer I hike, the lighter the load becomes. Provisions dwindle, stamina grows, and the desire to finish fortifies me. Besides, like much ecstasy, complete exhaustion wipes out the self, which can be a blessing. As long as I feed this engine and maintain its parts it will serve me well, and cheaper than others.

I do my best thinking while walking and find myself in good company. "I can only meditate when I am walking," Rousseau confessed. Kierkegaard insisted that he composed all his literary works on foot. An entire school of sages, the Greek Cynic philosophers, lived vagabond lives, berating the settled that stooped in the market places. (Diogenes, who might have slept in a wine barrel, thought Aristotle's legs were too skinny.) A walk down memory lane is not just metaphorical either—Charles Darwin acknowledged the mnemonic edge sauntering gives.

Topography structures cerebral cadences. Deep breaths perfuse thoughts. Footfalls beat a rhythm for language and song. In walking, the mind unkinks for its dialogue with nature, and the longer the walk, the deeper the dialogue. There is scientific truth to all this. Regular walkabouts improve memory and reduce depression, anxiety, and the risk of dementia. They keep you mentally spry. The semi-automatic, repetitive act leaves the creative part of the brain free to go gallivanting. Another bonus of thinking afoot, a pain-relieving side effect, is the distraction it offers from blisters and creaky joints.

One last advantage of backpacking as a form of locomotion comes from its leisurely pace. Human perception is attuned to, and evolved at, walking speed: three miles per hour. Walking, upright and long-distance, is the one physical skill at which we alone in the animal kingdom excel. It literally made us human. We walked out of Africa, to the ends of the Earth and have been unsettled ever since. The increasingly hectic pace with which we have altered ecosystems and the entire planet has been called "The Great Acceleration." It would behoove us to decelerate, as individuals and as a species.

Proceeding down-canyon, I pass through hot and cold air currents. With them come whiffs of cow and juniper berry backed by notes of stale water. A tarantula hawk, which is actually a kind of wasp, sails by, raising the hair on my neck. Anything this big should be a bird. Driving, you would miss such gems. The only insects you're likely to see explode bile-green on your windshield. Males of this neo-tropical wasp are content to siphon nectar from flowers. Females, which can become as big as my pinkie, look very attractive with their metallic-black rump and deep-amber wings. You expect them to buzz, but their approach is silent as an owl's, which makes them even more eerie. They are ruthless predators, true femmes fatales, but also good providers. No. They are what they are and should be: utterly alien despite any labels we pin on them. After mating, the female wasp locates the inhabited burrow of a tarantula or trapdoor spider. Twanging strands at the entrance, she summons the spider, an assassin ringing the doorbell. She then sinks her stinger into the homeowner and drags the paralyzed prey to her own lair, where she lays a single egg onto it. After hatching, the wasp larva feeds on the interred body until the time comes to transform itself, cocooned in silk. If female, the young wasp will unfurl diaphanous wings the following spring and take off on her own life-giving, search-and-destroy mission. This way of propagating may seem brutal, but it's part of the magnificent cycle that holds all living things.

Near the junction of the Paria Narrows and Buckskin Gulch afternoon gilds the shallows. Navajo sandstone folds into tight goosenecks in the stream's repeated attempt to break free. I pass Slide Rock, a silo-size chunk spalled from the cliffs. The Paria has whittled its base into a dainty pedestal, allowing hikers to walk underneath the slanted roof, between the rock and the canyon wall. Considering this smorgasbord of impressions, I wonder how "pedestrian" acquired the negative meanings "commonplace; prosaic or dull." "I am a pedestrian, nothing more," wrote Rimbaud, colorful walker of Abyssinia's desert.

A little later I drop my pack at the cavernous confluence to explore the lower end of the gulch. From Wire Pass, a slit in the Cockscomb's incline, it unspools more than twelve miles toward the Paria, as the longest and most spectacular and therefore most popular slot canyon on the Colorado Plateau. In some places, squeezing your shoulders, it soars 500 feet overhead. In others, you wade cesspools or fight quicksand. Its roseate walls funnel me to a boulder jumble, which I pass underground by crawling through a cubbyhole instead of climbing over it. Suddenly a feline face stares at me from the sand in front of my boot tips, eerily disembodied, a mask. Closer inspection reveals empty eye sockets, the muzzle, intact and with delicate whiskers, and patches of fur clinging to the browned skull. It's a bobcat, killed and dismembered perhaps by a flash flood. Here is another of the desert's many stories that will go untold for lack of witnesses or clear evidence.

Time dissolves as I move up the canyon. In a fit of "the bends," I just want to peek around the next bend, and the bend after that, and always one more. I keep walking as if under a spell.

Too soon, shadows lengthen inside the gulch, urging me to return to my pack and look for a tent site beyond the confluence. Before I reach camp, bats wing-stitch curlicues into peach twilight.

The next day I enter another, much shorter side canyon breaching the Paria's palisades. Its spring splashes emerald across a sere canvas, spreading reeds, scouring rushes, and mosses under box elder and cottonwood canopies. Countless leaf skeletons rustle on the twigs—spoil from some caterpillar invasion. Yellowing tamarisk filigree and a few daisies colored like faded lilacs betray the year's waning. Coral light caresses the gorge, glancing off planed, tilted sandstone.

The trail ends under Wrather Arch, a colossal vault sprung from striped walls at the head of this box canyon. Freezer-size chunks of its ceiling litter the incline, crude shavings from time's workbench. In all my canyon sojourns I have witnessed rocks falling only a few times, normally heard rather than seen—the geological clock beats at an inhuman pace. More reason to slow down and behold, to measure your own pace against that of the ages.

Until the Paria begins to grind down through Kayenta sand-and-siltstone the walking is easy, a stroll along a beach, not a strenuous canyon scramble. Instead of crushed seashells and kelp, juniper berries and pine needles limn the wrack line. Summer's thunderstorms swept them from the edge of the Paunsaugunt Plateau, the Pink Cliffs step of the topographical tiers known as the Grand Staircase. I set out on this trip to the lower, red-blond cliff band after the monsoon season to avoid pouncing floods. When I stoop by the river—a creek really, at this water level—frost rime on its margins turns out to be salt crystals blossoming from the ground.

For half a mile the staid streamlet perks up, hurdling across lavender ledges, pretending to be a rambunctious mountain brook. Squeezed by jagged terraces and talus, it surges between house rocks, forcing me to look for a dry route on the slopes. Hard to imagine that in 1871 sixty head of cattle were herded down this gash in the earth. How the walls must have rung with cows bawling at the land's bitterness! The first Anglo to stare dumbfounded at these features was John Doyle Lee, after the Mormon Church ordered him to establish a Colorado River ferry at the Paria's mouth.

Lee had been scapegoated for the Mountain Meadow Massacre during which a wagon train of settlers had been attacked and all adults killed. Reluctantly, the Latter-day renegade obeyed his call of duty: to stay out of sight. He disappeared for a spell into no-white-man's and no-white-woman's land, secure between scalloped parapets, and started the ferry business with a boat John Wesley Powell abandoned. U. S. marshals wanted him also for polygamy. In the course of an eventful life Lee married eighteen women, cohabiting, they say, with as many as five at a time.

Lee's exile ended in 1874, and three years later, excommunicated by then, he faced a firing squad for his involvement in the slaughter. His need for female companionship had tripped him up. He was arrested while visiting one of his wives. Emma Lee, wife number seventeen, kept operating the ferry until 1879, and then sold it. After three men drowned in a crossing in 1928 the ferry shut down and a bridge replaced it—one more step in the domestication of the Southwest.

Where the stream weasels past a final constriction, the scenery changes once again. Saltbush dapples the wide and parched valley. Soft hills of Chinle simmer rainbow-striped, wrinkled by rain. A subtle splendor infuses the strata transected by Utah Highway 89 and the Colorado's lazy loops, each layer responding in its signature way to the touch of erosion and light. Deeper and deeper, muscle tissue and bone peel away, revealing Earth's fine-grained anatomy, her innermost secrets.

In the lower canyon, petroglyphs scar rough-and-tumble colossi, testifying to the Paria's importance as a route to the Colorado long before Lee set foot on its banks. On one patinated giant at the foot of the slope only half of the images face right-side up. Sometimes in rock art the dead are depicted head-down, hanging in limbo. But most likely this boulder rolled before pre-Columbians had finished engraving its sides. Or a different bunch later came upon the toppled block. Its symbols and pointillist figures baffle us. Modern interpretations fail. The wild-sheep hunters that first combed these hollows did not distinguish between art and religion, between humans and non-humans, between the natural and the supernatural, or a rock and the world. They incised in stone what came to them in visions or dreams, what they saw or what they had heard in old stories, it did not matter which. If additional proof for the difference in mindsets is needed, consider which traveler now would chisel scorpions and centipedes into monoliths, and with flint burins only. Ours is an age of impatience, of destinations. To us moderns, Aldo Leopold wrote halfway in time between Lee and myself, that land is "the space between cities in which crops grow," and we bridge that space by car or plane. To the first people, the land upon which they walked was a source of strength.

Near sunset I arrive at Lonely Dell, John Doyle Lee's old homestead. The name still feels appropriate. Tan adobe melds with lion-skin desert. Crosses in the ranch cemetery lean into the evening. A nearby dugout, cobwebbed and dark as an animal's den, barely seems fit for human habitation. Past hopes, dreams, and cares, past hatreds and fears crumble in the shadows of ruins. The bobcat again vacantly gazes at me, another trailside *memento mori*. I wonder if Lee ever questioned the striving of a world, or the doctrine of a church, he'd temporarily left behind. I wonder if, in a chair on his porch, feet propped on the railing, he sometimes was simply content to watch the light on the cliffs change.

So Long, Promised Land

Tell me the landscape in which you live, and I will tell you who you are.

—ORTEGA Y GASSET

AS THE OLD YEAR FADES from view, I am busy boxing up things for my move to Alaska. Sifting through detritus accumulated over the years, I try to decide what is essential, what is too heavy or bulky, what can be left behind. Stacks of discolored photos quickly distract me from my task. Lost in reveries I shuffle these mementos of a love affair with the Colorado Plateau, an affair that began more than two decades ago.

I was exploring the Southwest in 1982, as a tourist. Smitten with the sublime light, the uncluttered space, the convoluted canyons and silk-and-steel rivers, I decided to live there some day. Life had other plans, but I kept gravitating toward the red rock gardens, where Moab became a haven of sorts. Eventually, I moved there for good. Following my conviction that a perfectly sized town is one in which everything, including wilderness, lies within easy walking or biking distance, I settled in Moab on the tail end of the uranium-mining boom. I felt fortunate, as this muscular and reclusive landscape became not only my home but also my workplace. During summers, I spent more days on the Colorado and its tributaries than in town. My working outfit as a river guide consisted of sandals and shorts. Peoples' faces often lit up with envy when I asked them to step into my "office," the raft.

Too soon, I became aware that the Promised Land, like many other places these days, suffered from industrial encroachment and greed. The West's troubled legacy revealed itself in cattle grazing the canyons inside a National Monument—"Escowlante." Thumper trucks explored for oil, destroying delicate soils and vegetation bordering Canyonlands National Park. Politicians supported proposals to extract and process oil shale along the Green River's marvelous Desolation Canyon. Commerce and people in garish outfits discovered my hideout, pronouncing Moab the Mountain Biking Capital of the West. For the longest time I denied living in a resort town, even when the annual Jeep Safari forced me and many other residents to flee town for a week, to avoid traffic and the attendant mayhem.

In synch with rising visitor numbers, the wealthy started to buy second homes in town. Property prices and taxes rose accordingly, forever placing the dream of a little shack of my own beyond reach. The cost of some frou-frou coffee drinks soon began to equal half the hourly wage dirt bags and river rats like me made in service industry jobs, naturally without benefits. Moab lacked a shoe repair place, affordable health care and housing, a food co-op, noise control.... Instead it sprouted real estate offices, T-shirt and "art" boutiques, motels and gas stations, jeep, bike, and boat rentals. Mountain and road bikers rubbed sweaty shoulders with hikers, climbers, jeepers, base jumpers, skydivers, kayakers, rafters, golfers, and vintage car lovers. They all rubbed my nerve endings raw. They drank dry the bars, clogged the river and canyons. The off season, welcomed by many locals as a change of pace and reminder of why they had chosen this town in the first place, shrank year by year, cropped at both ends by mountain unicycle festivals and other bogus events. It got harder and harder to escape unwanted company in the Best of Beyond. I often wished my domicile could be famous (if famous it must be) for record-breaking pumpkins or the nation's oldest hay barn.

Revisiting a favorite haunt in the Escalante watershed the first time in ten years, I was appalled by the changes. Foot trails cut through cryptobiotic soil carpets, betraying people's laziness, their need to shortcut across canyon meanders. They had not simply trampled single tracks but whole networks into each knobby surface. Some morons had clearly misread the BLM's plea to leave behind nothing but footprints. At popular campsites, which appeared strangely denuded even for this arid country, wooden signs directed visitors to pit toilets installed—and hope-fully emptied—by monument staff. The voices of nearby camp-ers echoed around slickrock bends, undermining the privacy I had hoped for. Aluminum pull-tabs and charcoal from illegal campfires had replaced the arrowhead fragments, potsherds, and centuries-old corncobs once safe in alcove vaults. On Cedar Mesa, cameras now eyed ruins and rock art, trying to catch vandals in the act. Elsewhere, fences guarded petroglyph panels, and walkways channeled tour groups.

Faced with these changes, I realized for the first time that too many hikers degrade a wild place as easily and permanently as do too many cows. While it seems obvious and convenient to point fingers at off-road vehicle drivers, any sentient biped will have to admit that he or she is part of the problem. *Homo ambulans*, too, leaves nothing but traces and often takes peace and quiet from the backcountry.

The ecological concept of "carrying capacity" denotes a landscape's ability to sustain a particular number of organisms, depending on their foraging techniques or food requirements. Without irrigation, deserts support small bands of hunters and gatherers better than they do high concentrations of sedentary agriculturalists. Throughout this canyon country the crop now largely consists of tourists, and public lands managers still struggle to establish acceptable levels for recreational uses. Acceptable for whom, I wonder. Grand Canyon National Park's 2006 Colorado River Management Plan increased non-commercial user days by almost one third, trying to appease private boaters at the expense of mountain lions, bighorn sheep, silence, and solitude. And private boaters are still unhappy, clamoring for more. An already overtaxed "resource" is stretched to the limits. The park's zoning system, regulating backcountry hiking permits, is still rare on the Colorado Plateau. According to this allocation, a limited and seemingly justifiable quota of overnight permits is issued per zone. When filled, hikers have either to wait for openings or else settle for a less popular destination. With high visitor numbers in the spring and fall, the National Park Service and other agencies face a conundrum: to channel use and impact into fewer areas, or to spread it evenly over the lands entrusted to their care. In short, land managers accept that there will have to be "sacrifice zones."

But even official closures of fragile places mean little in a culture lacking respect and restraint. Years ago, the author of several self-published guidebooks praised one southeastern Utah gorge as "the gem of Canyonlands." Informed by the expert, people flocked to that sandstone cleft. (If you have only a weekend, you want to make sure it counts. No time to waste on mere two-star attractions.) Soon after, the Park Service decided to close the canyon, the only one that had never been grazed by livestock and as such gave a valuable baseline for assessing impact on the park's grazed districts. Hikers still go there, now for the extra zest of forbidden fruit.

Unfortunately, national glossies with circulation numbers as large as city populations hook affluent vacationers with paradoxical promises like *The Ten Least Known But Most Scenic Hikes of the xxx*—insert your favorite wilderness here. One rag even includes GPS coordinates for "points of interest," read: sensitive areas. While we gain certainty with electronic plotting devices, we are losing much. Biologists reported that, after one feature ran in that magazine, visitor numbers in Yellowstone's *xyz* Valley multiplied, and that the resident wolf pack temporarily left its home range.

Even the Four Corners' Navajo reservation, which long had been spared the worst excess, perhaps due to its "Third World feel" and user-unfriendly permit system, now suffers tourism's side effects. A few canyons became accessible with guides only, after a flash flood killed eleven visitors, possibly to avoid costly search-and-rescue missions or even more expensive liability suits; about a dozen more canyons were recently closed to all outsiders. Sadly, non-Navajos hiking without permits, harassing livestock, littering, and disturbing archaeological ruins brought on these closures.

For years, I was still content to take paying customers down rivers and canyons. But I slowly realized that many, if not most of them, were only after the glossy skin, not the meat and bones, or, heavens forbid, the soul of a place. They considered wilderness a sort of outdoor gym-cum-tanning salon, a thrill ride with a picnic on the side, pretty scenery to write home about, or perhaps worst of all, just another checkmark on their bucket list of "adventures." I've since heard of people who try to visit all fifty-nine U. S. national parks in fifty-nine days. My suggestion to them: spend fifty-nine days in one park—Grand Canyon or Gates of the Arctic. You might truly learn something.

One Moab river company did not hire me, because I was too outspoken in my "environmental convictions." Vacationers did not want to hear about mining or overgrazing or hydroelectric dams. They wanted rapids. They wanted fun. They wanted gourmet food, horseshoe games, solar showers, and, if possible, sleeping cots on the riverbank, or a little "canyon magic"—to hook up with a blonde river guide. The manager told me I would set a bad example for the younger guides and that his company was "pro-growth." Later I heard that a luxury tourism conglomerate had swallowed the outfit.

The former Moabite and critic of industrial tourism, Edward Abbey, named the spiritual price paid by those who depend on it for their livelihood: "They must learn the automatic smile." I had a hard time with that, though it cost me some tips and the goodwill of my boss.

I reached the low point of my guiding life during a Marlboro Adventure Team trip, an event for winners of a contest to promote smoking and rugged individualism in countries in which advertising for tobacco products was still legal. I prepared myself for trouble when I saw the trip leader remove the motor rig's spare outboard from its box, which he then filled with booze and tarry coffin nails. The organizers wanted us to flip boats in the whitewater, to provide the cameramen on shore with footage for commercials aired in South America. Between rapids, they asked the paddle-raft guides to tie on to a motor rig that dragged boatloads of macho, hung-over, helmeted conquistadors to the next "cool" spot.

Worst of all, though, I sensed, no, I *knew* I was part of the problem. My writing about the Four Corners' besieged landscapes seemed to make little positive difference; simply educating the public would never provide a cure. As my Coyote Gulch visit had shown, the lofty goal of teaching backcountry users about wilderness ethics and etiquette is based upon optimism with regards to human nature. Defaced rock art, scorched campfire rings, torn-out Wilderness Study Area markers, and fouled waterholes in even the most remote quarter quickly put dampers on such enthusiasm. I could not rid myself of the feeling that, by publicizing this region, I ultimately contributed to its defilement and destruction.

An argument can be made that public lands need to be used

recreationally to ensure their continued protection and funding, to keep them from rapacious developers or corrupt politicos. On the other hand, more than three million visitors per year might easily enjoy the Grand Canyon to death. There are no easy solutions to this dilemma.

Some of the boxes that will hold desert keepsakes still have old addresses on them; I think half of all my belongings must be in transit or storage at any given time. When I see the labels, more bittersweet memories come rushing in. I'm reliving the anticipation and reluctance I felt when shipping these boxes off. Disenchanted with academic life at the postgraduate level, unwilling to objectify cultures, and unable to secure grant money for my PhD project, I'd dropped out of school. There were few guide openings at the time for someone with limited experience and much competition for them. Opportunity called elsewhere, seconded by the desert's siren song—I'd been offered an outdoor instructor position in a youth program in Arizona. With my moorings already cut, I followed the current. The rest is river history.

I am aware that moving to Alaska is not a solution. The political climate in the Big Dipper State closely resembles that of the Beehive State. As a latter-day itinerant, I will become part of the problem there—it can't be avoided. But approaching middle age, I feel that time is running out. To paraphrase Aldo Leopold, I simply don't wish to grow old without wild country to be old in.

While moving to Alaska in mid-winter seems unwise, I cannot think of a better place to start the New Year, or a new chapter in life. Let it be cold. Let it be dark. Let summers be buggy. And let us hope we can keep some places wild.

North

I listened to the chiming of the ice. It was just a moment in the mountains, but enough moments add up to a life.

—DOUGLAS CHADWICK, *The Wolverine Way* (2012)

Blacktop Cuisine

"**D**INNER IS READY, GUYS." We pulled our chairs to the kitchen table, as Bart Blankenship took a bubbling casserole from the oven. The fragrance of *masa*, chilies, and cilantro suffused the room.

"Looks great," I said, forking up my first bite. The meat was a bit stringy, with a gamey tang to it. "What is it?"

"Bobcat tamales," Bart said. Furry white eyebrows wiggled up his forehead like caterpillars, accentuating the trademark Blankenship smirk.

"Where did you get this, Bart?"

"Oh, outside of Pagosa. At first I thought it was a Standard Poodle."

"Hmmm. Interesting," I said, taking another, more tentative bite. Not what I imagined cat to taste like. And not "like chicken" at all.

My friend and former roommate Bart is an Information Age mountain man. Before he bought a boat to sail the Seven Seas, he worked for Outward Bound and sometimes for an outdoor survival school in southern Utah. With his ex-wife he authored a book about flint knapping and other Stone Age skills. His chert and bottle-glass arrowheads were not just functional—they were works of art. He wove fishing nets from home-processed yucca fibers and taught his children to catch trout with bare hands, much to the dismay of their summer-camp counselors. Bart's idea of dressing up for a night on the town was to don his brain-tanned buckskin shirt and pants. I never knew what would show up in our freezer from day to day.

Like other aficionados, Bart became a road-kill gourmet by default. As the founder of a school for primitive skills, he needed furs, hides, feathers, antlers, and sinew in order to teach tanning, arrow fletching, and tool hafting. Outside of Alaska, highways seemed like the best places to procure these materials. Bart started by calling the Colorado DOT for recent deer kills, and there were usually a few in the Boulder vicinity. Skinning the carcasses, Bart found that much of the meat was still good. A frugal guy who hates waste, he began to take these scraps home. Generally, Bart is not too concerned about ticks, rabies, or tularemia—"rabbit fever." He washes his hands and any meat thoroughly and otherwise thinks that a dose of bacteria will keep his immune system strong. When in doubt, he has a surefire way of testing road kill. "I cook a small piece without seasoning and taste it. If it tastes like it was dipped in vinegar then it's still okay and likely won't make you sick. But my kids won't eat it, and so I leave it."

As a parent of three with little income, Bart was quick to point out the economic aspect of eating road kill. Since the 1980s, he supplemented his family's larder with deer, elk, and bobcat. At times, up to a third of the meat consumed by the Blankenships came from fender benders. At thirty to fifty pounds of usable meat per deer and a store value of two to five dollars per pound, the savings were substantial. But unlike some of my dirtbag river guide friends, Bart drew the line at Dumpster-diving, which he considered gross.

A roster of Bart's "trophies" read like a *Who's Who* of western wildlife. My friend admitted to having boiled and eaten a great horned owl once. "I ran it over and felt I had to do something with it," he said. But generally, he set aside the "exotics"—coyote, raccoon, fox, opossum, wild hog, otter, badger, and rattlers—to make hatbands, mittens, or arrow quivers.

The legalities, as well as the actual experience, of peeling bunnies off the asphalt can be Byzantine. While Bart dodged traffic to avoid suffering his dinner's fate, he did well to remember federal and state laws. It is illegal, for example, to collect certain animals, from the road or elsewhere. Only Native Americans with a religious permit are allowed to possess an eagle feather. The state of Utah issues a permit each time an individual wants to retrieve a killed animal. And whereas motorists in Arizona are entitled to keep meat from a deer they have hit, the same act can land you in prison in Oregon. On long road trips, scrounging could become quite an ordeal. Bart remembered one outing in particular. "We were driving in Kansas and had four Raccoons in bags tied to the roof, and they were thawing, and blood was dripping down the windows. We found we weren't allowed to have them in Kansas, even though we picked them up elsewhere. So we ended up beating it back to Colorado where they'd be legal." Another time, Bart's youngest son got carsick and threw up in his seat next to half a fox his dad was transporting. On the bright side, the mess got them out of a citation for speeding.

Even at his home, the Law kept an eye on Bart's preparations. He recalled the time a concerned neighbor alerted the authorities. "The EPA came and asked where our toxic chemicals were for tanning the hides. When we showed them the buckets of brains, they said we might want to keep a lid on to keep out the flies. The Department of Wildlife came, while we were using a ceiling fan to dry some furs; but they left with a brochure of our primitive skills school. The fire department came when we smoked hides but went away when they saw the smoke coming out of our wood stove and going straight into a deer hide. The City of Boulder came and left, and so did the police."

While Bart may strike some people as eccentric or a throw-back to fur rendezvous times, more and more Americans are discovering the potential of road kill. Taxidermists fix flattened pelts for natural history museum exhibits. A gallery owner in South Dakota plucks porcupine quills to fashion into jewelry. A New Mexico sculptress and tattoo artist assembles bones into motorcycles or "Gnarleys." An Arizona state biologist prepares skulls and other skeletal parts to be used as educational kits in schools. Frozen corpses serve him as models for scientific illustrations; fresher meat ends up on the barbecue grill or feeding his boas and pythons.

Despite their entertainment value and utility, creative uses of road kill can hardly disguise the social and ecological costs daily incurred on U.S. highways. Aside from abetting habitat fragmentation, pollution, and noise, roads take a more direct, bloody toll on biodiversity. Vehicles kill hundreds of millions of animals every year. Snakes and amphibians, including many endangered species, take the brunt of this onslaught. Toad tunnels or pronghorn overpasses can limit casualties and keep biotopes connected. But sometimes, they bring new hardships. Toads migrating in Davis, California, refused to enter a tunnel built for them, because it was dark. When the town installed lighting, they dried out and died. Birds wised up to this all-you-can-eat, awaiting toads that emerged at the tunnel's mouth. Not even our national parks are safe. On Yellowstone's roads alone, 1,559 large mammals died between 1989 and 2003. But the boundary between victims and perpetrators becomes blurred. Two hundred people died last year in about 250,000 collisions with animals. The average repair of an automobile damaged by deer (or more often, by reckless driving) runs around 2,000 dollars.

Perhaps, like our fellow creatures, we humans are not hard-wired for life in the fast lane. Neither, some critics insist, were we meant to consume carrion.

Simply the thought of eating possum paella or rattlesnake ragout will induce dry heaves in most people. Yet the widespread prejudice against scavenging only masks humble origins. It is a credo, a pretense akin to the convert's denial of obsolete pagan practices. The vile reality may be hard to stomach: gleaning is in our genes. It helped us become who we are.

The concept of Man the Hunter (and by extension Woman the Gatherer) is not entirely the product of gender biases ruling science or politics. It also appears as a case of mythmaking by a species in search of dignity, a species still largely intent on seeing itself as the apex of, if not separated from, the animal world. *Nature* is red in tooth and claw. *We* are sticklers for table manners, devoted to fancy cooking. Truth told, rather than wielding spears and skewering African mammoths, *Homo sapiens* began its career as a beggar in nature's soup kitchen. Opportunists with big brains, our hominid ancestors on the savanna stuffed their faces with leftovers wrangled from lion or leopard kills, in competition with hyenas, jackals, and vultures. In an eat-or-be-eaten world, bone picking proved to be more efficient than gathering (especially when protein yield is compared), yet less risky than hunting—an optimal foraging strategy. In this scenario, the invention of stone tools later gave us an edge over other scavengers by facilitating dismemberment, as well as marrow and brain extraction. (Which can be tough with fingernails and underdeveloped dentition.) Speech and cooperation quickly followed, in turn giving birth to more complex behaviors like big game hunting and presidential campaigning.

Supposedly, anthropology can even shed light on the rank reputation of blacktop cuisine. Evolutionary psychologists speculate that our revulsion at eating dead and rotten things (as opposed to just rotten things, like Limburger cheese) developed as an adaptive trait. This sort of "intuitive microbiology" helped early hominids to avoid lethal cases of food poisoning. Physical anthropologists, on the other hand, like to point out that, even under an equatorial sun, it can take up to forty-eight hours until flesh begins to putrefy. Furthermore, carcasses produced by "natural" death are likely to be free of dangerous parasites, because most such deaths result from malnutrition rather than from disease. Good news for the harvesters of ditches and interstates.

In my new home state Alaska the road kill menu is less varied than Bart's backyard fare. As if to compensate, everything is super-sized here, including the servings. (An adult, 1,100 pound moose normally yields about 700 pounds of meat, meat that is much leaner and more nutritious than beef.) Trains and vehicles annihilate about 820 moose, carnage only surpassed in Sweden, where motorists cull moose populations by four to six thousand animals each year. About 120 moose annually fall prey to the Alaska Railroad's yellow-and-blue engines. With a sense of humor honed at fifty-below-zero temperatures, residents of this state call the train between Fairbanks and Anchorage "the Moose Butcher." When northern lights play above snowdrifts, animals follow the plowed tracks for lack of easier trails. Allegedly, bull moose even take on locomotives, as they would rack-sporting competitors during the fall rut. Heavy snowfalls and overcrowding can drive the animals into urban areas, leading to more fatalities. Occasionally, the quick hand of transportation technology also cuts short the lives of black bears, Dall's sheep, and mountain goats. Sixteen-hour nights and icy roads result in tons of high-quality foodstuff: prime cuts, tender loin, spare ribs, and minced meat. And at subarctic temperatures, this bonanza does not easily spoil.

Bountiful as the biblical supper of bread loaves and fish, "Bullwinkle chili" from a single moose feeds close to 400 mouths at a soup kitchen. Alaska's urban and semi-urban centers have therefore implemented programs to retrieve and distribute road kill to the needy. In Anchorage, Fairbanks, the Matanuska-Susitna Valley, and on the Kenai Peninsula, hundreds of charities and individuals benefit from low visibility, speeding, drunk driving, and poor road conditions or reflexes. Nearly all road-kill moose in the state goes to nonprofit organizations, many of which are churches. Beneficiaries must respond within thirty minutes to a coordinator's call to salvage the meat. If they fail to do so, the follower-up on a list will be given a chance. Alaska Fish and Game biologists or hunters affiliated with the nonprofits often are called upon to shoot wildlife injured in accidents.

Eileen Brooks is the road kill coordinator for the Anchorage region and Mat-Su Borough of south-central Alaska. Colleagues refer to her as the "Queen of the Gut Pile." But according to Eileen, the Blankenship diet alleviates hardship in a place where the cost of living is high. "A lot of people can't afford to buy steaks or even hamburger," she says. And while many Alaskans reap the fruits of subsistence hunting and fishing, these are not options for the urban poor. Luckily (for them), in Eileen's area alone, 100 nonprofits are signed up for road kill in a typical winter, and some community churches receive an average of ten moose a year.

A major tenet of sustainable living admonishes us not just to recycle but also to curb wastefulness in the first place. Unfortunately, a society obsessed with driving is unlikely to ever fully embrace measures that reduce wildlife mortality on its roads. Speed limits, better signage, fencing, or animal overpasses all could prevent unnecessary deaths. Tight budgets and narrow minds, however, ensure that ecological attrition will continue. Short of all-out solutions, we can at least honor the casualties with a token gesture. Sharing the mangled flesh in a form of unholy communion, we acknowledge their sacrifice. So, let us show some respect. Let's neaten our highways a bit. Let us break the mold of culinary routine. To connoisseurs sick of French, Thai, or Mexican, Bart recommends the chef's special: grille gopher in crankcase oil, with a side of creamed coyote—guaranteed to tickle the palate while sparing the wallet. Do yourselves a favor, though, and skip the muskrat mush.

Bon appétit!

In the Wake of Skin Boats

WITH HER ENGINES CUT, *Steller* idles inside Bear Cove, a crook in the coastline of Kenai Fjords National Park, while we unload our sea-kayaks from the stern. A low-angle sun ignites the sea and shore as if filtered through gold-tinted glass. Where the high tide meets hemlock and spruce, not a foot of level ground is left. We don't know what the green wall conceals. But the coast that one Park Service historian called rock-bound and stern shows a welcoming face on this summer day.

Initially the newcomers thought they had found a virgin world. When slender boats fashioned from animal skins crowded their ships, they quickly realized that this coast had been home to people for thousands of years. The Pacific Eskimos now known as Alutiit called themselves Sugpiat, the "real people," though Russian fur hunters and traders considered them to be subhuman. Despite their disdain, the colonizers came to admire the native "leathern canoes" for their elasticity. They complimented their speed and considered them safer in bad weather than European small boats. With the help of indigenous paddlers who powered these broad-beamed, shallow craft up shrouded estuaries and into lagoons, the word of God spread nearly as fast as did trade goods.

A smooth three-hour ride delivered our group, two instructors and six Outward Bound students, in Aialik Bay. The boat ride spared us paddling nearly forty miles up Resurrection Bay, around a wave-lashed promontory with few landing places. *Steller*'s observation deck also gave us views of parrot-billed puffins clipping the spray, of mist geysering from the slick, glossy spine of some whale, and of a large sea otter—ninety pounds of bewhiskered curiosity reclining in our wave train.

In days long gone, otters learned to fear humans. People closely related to the Alutiit have lived in the Kodiak Archipelago and Prince William Sound, and on the Lower Kenai and Southern Alaska Peninsula where it tapers into the Aleutian chain, for at least 7,000 years. They chased seals and sea otters in ingenious kayaks and lived in pit houses roofed with driftwood and sod. From the mid-eighteenth century on, under Russian supervision, they served the demands of Asian markets, driving sea otters, which have the thickest fur of any animal on Earth, to the brink of extinction. Each April, Alutiit assembled for commercial hunts, in fleets of up to 500 *baidarkas* (a Russian term for Alutiiq *qayat* or "kayaks;" singular: *qayaq*). Led by *promyshlenniki*—traders that more closely resembled mercenaries—the fragile-looking boats would travel east from Kodiak Island, along the outer Kenai coast, to Sitka and pick up additional hunters on the way. Crashing otter populations eventually made the hunt unprofitable, and with the pressure gone, the species recovered remarkably well.

Our group's excitement is almost palpable, and the long hours of daylight and heady Alaska wilderness energize us. Riding the wave of euphoria, I teach a brief lesson on campsite selection and leave-no-trace ethics before we tackle the gear piles on the beach. We are in our bags by ten thirty, tired but still wired from the first day's impressions.

After breakfast and with the weather holding, we get down to basics: kayak anatomy, paddle strokes, and the much-dreaded wet exit and reentry. The water is cold, though not by Alaska standards. A few of the less motivated students try to talk their way out of the drill. But after a reminder that it is not negotiable and a demonstration by their instructors, they all follow suit. Two students, Chris and Jake, take several attempts to flip their big double kayak. Upon reentry they capsize again, because Chris, already back in the cockpit, forgets to lean to the opposite side when six-foot-three Jake struggles onto the deck. My co-instructor Josh and I grin at each other. Before this trip is over all of us will be forced out of our comfort zone. These two students have just been introduced to one of the Outward Bound pillars: teamwork.

The training of Alutiiq kayakers started even earlier, at age fourteen. On calm days boys would travel into the bays to catch fish or kill birds with throw darts. A game of skill improved their hand-eye coordination. Sitting on the ground as if in a kayak, one youth would throw fletched, metal-tipped miniature darts at an animal carving that another swung in front of him on a string. Elders encouraged the neophytes to harden their bodies by taking dips in the ocean at dawn. Calisthenics kept them balanced and flexible. Pull-ups on the roof rafters of their homes padded their shoulders and forearms with muscle. At sixteen, having undergone cleansing rituals, they joined uncles and other maternal kinsmen on sea-otter-hunting excursions. When they encountered a raft of otters, hunters would slap the water with their paddles, forcing the animals to dive until they became exhausted and breathless. Speed and accuracy mattered; an otter belonged to the first man who wounded it.

Hieromonk Gideon, an Orthodox official whom Empress

Catherine the Great sent to report on Russian America in 1803, vividly described the methods and skills Kodiak Islanders employed in hunting sea otters from double-hatch boats:

> The first man who sights a sea otter signals the others by lifting his paddle. The others try to encircle the place at a distance within range of their spears. Only those who occupy the forward hatches throw the spears, everyone at will, before each other, while those in the rear hatches maneuver the *baidarkas*. Sometimes, the sea otter is hit by two spears, and in such a case, the carcass belongs to the hunter whose spear struck the animal closer to the head or above the other spear.

A lone hunter caught in a storm could stabilize his *qayaq* by tying inflated seal bladders to its sides. Perhaps he had learned by observing otters, which, caught in a gale, wrap kelp strips around their middles to ride out the commotion anchored and buoyed. Boys also were taught early to Eskimo-roll, righting capsized *qayat* while seal-intestine parkas cinched to the cockpit kept them dry. Unfortunately, with only twelve days on this course, our students won't master this advanced self-rescue technique.

Assured that our pod can travel safely, at least under present conditions, we head out for the day. While the students work on staying in formation, we cruise by several sea caves, dark mouths in the land's escarpments. Closer to shore, the barely perceptible swell becomes animated, the ocean's rise and fall echoing in rock cavities like wet pounding and deep breathing. An offshore breeze carries the scent of fecundity: a cocktail of salt, fish, forest, mud, and decay. Wary of rebounding waves, we keep our distance from barnacled boulders and the kelp beds that hide them.

Later, at camp, we inventory our food supply under much

joking and laughter. We stay up late telling stories and, by re-hashing the past, shape the present and forge bonds that, we hope, will weather the future.

As is typical for this stretch of coastline, the next day turns drizzly. We paddle ten miles to Abra Cove. A student captain and two navigators lead, trying to keep the group tight. How strange, I surprise myself thinking, for land creatures to travel this smoothly this far without gaining or losing elevation. Propelled by paddle cadences, the bows of our boats slice the slate-gray surface like Roman galleys.

Our double bladed, concave, and offset "feathered" paddles optimally transmit muscle power to water; they also prevent one-sided exertion. The Alutiit mostly used paddles with a single leaf-shaped "spearhead" blade. This blade—thinning at the edges, and often decorated with black and red ocher—was specifically engineered for windy conditions and quick stabiliz-ing maneuvers. Beyond mere means of propulsion, the paddle served as a kind of sonar: hunters would clench the grip between their teeth, with the blade in the ocean. They could sense game moving underwater through the wood's vibration as if reading land animal tracks in fresh snow.

In a cove gliding by on starboard we notice three black bear cubs. They are engaged in a wrestling match, now standing on hind legs, now dropping on all fours to chase each other across the beach. Mom is nowhere in sight. Bald eagles scrutinize us from trees bearded with pale-green moss. In a flurry of fins and tails, salmon prepare for their inland migration. Harbor seals raise their heads from the sea like puppies watching a parade. We travel through galaxies of jellyfish. A creation myth tells of the first Alutiit falling from the sky in their kayaks, and I understand how they must have felt: travellers between worlds, released from physical limitations.

The tide's broad back carries us into the cove.

We pitch our tents on a storm-built gravel dam that defends marsh against ocean. A thousand-foot cliff lines the back of the bay; cascading waterfalls have stained it rust red, the minerals, complemented by splashes of burnt-orange lichen.

During dinner we watch another black bear. This one is grazing in the meadow behind camp. Absolutely unconcerned by our presence, it forages just a stone's throw away from the tents. That's a little too close for comfort. Shouting and waving, we announce ourselves. Without hurrying or altering its course, the animal continues its evening rounds and eventually saunters into the bushes. The students are awed. Most of them have never seen a bear in the wild.

Fueled by a pot of hot oatmeal we shove off again the next morning. Soon, brash ice signals the terminus of Aialik Glacier. Tinkling like ice cubes in a drink mixes with the fizzing of air bubbles released from the vise of the eons, each one a tiny time capsule. Bergy bits migrate from the bay on the tide, stately Pleistocene beasts bound for oblivion. Growlers the size of beer kegs jostle our kayaks with deep *thunk*s, forcing us into single file. The point kayak as icebreaker clears a channel for our flotilla.

The thunder of avalanche or volcanic eruption rolls across the water with each glacier calving. We slip behind Squab Island about a mile from the interface of the sea and Aialik's tumultuous front. Shielded from rogue waves caused by collapsing ice towers, we grab a quick snack rafted up in our boats. Thousands of kittiwakes protest our presence. The mob lifts in a vortex of wings and piercing cries but quickly settles again.

We notice ice floes in the bay, haul-outs for harbor seals, in particular mothers and pups. Remote video monitoring has shown that seals flee the ice when tour boats approach, or even kayakers. The animals experience stress, and more disturbingly, pups can get trampled in a panic. In Aialik, Glacier Bay, and Prince William Sound, harbor seals are in decline. With the recent recession of many tidewater glaciers, their resting, birthing, nursing, and molting platforms have diminished. Forced onto shore, seals and especially pups become easy meals for wolves or bears combing the beaches.

To the Alutiit, harbor seals, and Steller's sea lions, were as bison to the Plains Indians; and the *qayaq* was their horse. The fin-footed mammals nourished Alutiiq hunters and their families with meat, blubber, and oil, kept them clothed, and their homes warm and lit. They inspired song, story, dance, and ritual, totemic connections for an entire society. Human and non-human lives merged in the bottleneck of survival, in a way of life sanctioned by taboos and mutual obligations. This relationship found expression in material culture, such as oil lamps sculpted from beach cobbles and lit during ceremonies. Seal heads joined to human faces peered up from the lamp bottoms as oil was burning off, symbols of shared fates, of porous boundaries, common origins. In more mundane, though no less astonishing transformations, sealskins became vehicles in which to trade, visit, and hunt. Five or six large skins of spotted seal or young sea lion sheathed a single *qayaq*. Boat-builders preferred the hides of female sea lions, which were thinner and more pliable; they also have fewer scars and holes compared to the hides of the more combative males.

Beaching our craft near the glacier's southwestern flank, we find that the closest campsite lies about 200 yards from shore. It takes all hands to haul the fully loaded double into the moraine's moonscape of grit, beyond the sea's reach.

A short hike along the stair-stepped glacier leads to benches spangled with wildflowers, and further rewards us with a raven's-eye view across the bay and into the ranks of mountains. Farther up the bay, Skee Glacier caps solemn, gray heights. Aialik is merely one of over thirty named ice worms that inch down from the vast Harding Ice Field—actually, most of them now hotfoot it in reverse. McCarty Glacier retreated fifteen miles in the last 100 years. The metaphor "glacial pace" no longer works. The ice field itself has thinned about seventy feet since Fats Domino sang *Blueberry Hill*. It nevertheless is difficult to imagine this crystalline weight, the carapace at the peninsula's heart: 700 square miles of ice 3000 feet thick.

On our return to the foot of Aialik, we don't see any berries bluing the heather, but I still find my thrill contemplating the ice-choked bay from up high: this glacier still reaches the sea. Back at camp, we build a rare fire below the tide line. Half a forest of driftwood lies scattered about like bones of some Brobdingnagian race, and the evening promises to be cool. Already, winds falling daily from the gray-and-white waste at our backs spin glacial silt between the tents. Perhaps the fire will help offset the chill of this flint-skinned hermit coast. Local trees, though never driftwood, furnished the skeleton of a *qayaq* in an elegant welding of the land and sea's bounties. Native artisan-craftsmen used hemlock for the frame, and spruce for the stem, stern, and crosspieces. They knew their materials as well as they knew the sea. Hemlock cracks or breaks easily; spruce is drier, and ribs from it can be bent after steaming. Besides tanning and sewing many a frame's skin cover, women gathered and split spruce roots, which could replace sinew as the boat's lashings. According to the Alutiiq artist and seamstress June Simeonoff Pardue, men often made their own boat covers, because their life depended on them. If their craftsmanship lacked, their seams leaked, they had no one to blame but themselves.

Due to the suppleness of its joints, a *qayaq* could absorb the ocean's thrashing; rather than bounce atop wave crests it slithered over them, a piloted snake. Such boats also were lighter than dugout canoes and could be carried without much effort. Alutiiq woodworkers still fashion kayaker bentwood hats from thin spruce planks. Now largely works of art, these over-size duckbills once were essential headwear. Like our visors or baseball hats, they keep the rain from a paddler's face and cut the glare from a low sun. Painted with bright geometric designs and adorned with puffin beaks, seal whiskers, or feathers, they not only conveyed status but also hid the hunter's identity from his prey—important when spirits retaliate for breaking any taboo in a maze of so many.

Throughout a night of twilight, we hear the glacier flex in its stone trough; distant skirmishing, cracking rifles and booming cannon, assails our dreams.

On day six, we emerge from our tents into a world of fine rain. The forest has become one dripping grotto. All peaks have been blotted out. On my way to the kitchen for coffee, I run into Josh, his red-apple cheeks flushed with glee. "Come here," he says. "I have to show you something." One of the kayaks has been moved. A life jacket has been tossed aside and left on the ground. Hatch covers are mud-smeared. My co-instructor points to the deck, to a paw print with five toe pads. Black bear! Fortunately, all our food still dangles from a rope strung between two trees. "Look at this," Josh says, finally sputtering. My boat's mascot rubber chicken (it lays an egg when you squeeze it) has been decapitated.

"That's not funny," I say. "It was brand new."

Reverence for the kayak, grown from the fact that you entrust your life to it, connects us to the Alutiit on some deeper level. We personalize our polyurethane tubes with hand-painted names and lucky charms; they daubed their boats with red bands and seams tasseled with seal whiskers and dyed bits of wool. They strapped implements of survival onto their decks—seal clubs, bailers, lances, or harpoons, throwing-boards, darts, bows and arrow-filled quivers—all within easy reach and crucial as our map cases, compasses, bilge pumps. Like us, they carried spare paddles and patch kits to mend tears in the hull.

After wrestling soaked tents and tarps into our kayak hatches, we enjoy the crossing to Verdant Cove. Sun dispels the clouds, turning the sea a Caribbean blue and Verdant Island's bulk a tropical green, a perfect hideout for mutineers. On the cobble beach, we pull out our wet gear to dry. The scene reminds Josh of a yard sale. "Looks more like a shipwreck," I say.

With our stuff securely weighed down by rocks, Josh takes us on a short hike. The foreshore resembles an old burn site: silvery trunks stripped of bark, the standing dead cushioned by billowy grass at their feet. Surprisingly, there is not much downed timber around. Ghost forests like this also haunt other parts of south-central Alaska's coast, reminding locals of one of the state's most dramatic upheavals, the Good Friday earthquake of March 27, 1964. Lasting less than five minutes, it registered 9.2 on the Richter scale, which at the time made it the second-strongest quake ever recorded. Swaths of destruction spread from the epicenter near Unakwik Inlet, leaving despair and 143 killed. Buildings in Anchorage cracked open like eggshell, spilling out panicked residents; streets buckled before ripping and swallowing cars; a massive underwater landslide sucked the Port Valdez docks into Prince William Sound. Old Chenega, the longest-occupied Alutiiq settlement in the sound ceased to exist when a twenty-seven foot tsunami drowned a third of its residents. Until that day, they'd had a good life and a reputation as great sea-mammal hunters. They were "soaked in grease," their neighbors said. Here in Aialik, waves from submarine slides surged 100 feet up the slopes at the bay's head, snapping spruce trees as wide as basketball hoops. Tidal pulses reached even Hawaii and Japan. Earth hiccupped, and tremors rippled worldwide.

When the convulsions stopped, topography had been rear-ranged, a repeat of a similar event in 1170 CE. This time, some areas around Kodiak had been pushed up thirty feet. Others, southeast of Anchorage, at the head of Cook Inlet, dropped as much as eight feet. In many places where shorelines subsided, as in Verdant Cove, roots siphoned saltwater from the ocean and trees died soon after. But the brine also preserved them, keeping them upright for these past forty years.

The ghost forest, however, is not the true destination of our hike, and we continue. Beyond the spiked perimeter, green envelops us in varying jungle shades. Leaf shadows dapple the forest floor, quivering in the breeze. We march single-file, silently following Josh on an overgrown path. The matted decay of the seasons muffles our steps. Barely glimpsed birds flit through the canopy. Inside this arbor, the sea's gentle falling-on-shore sounds like lisping. The trees, mostly alder and birch, tangle with berry brambles and mosses. Their girth, from wrist to bicep thickness, indicates second growth. No echo of people seems to linger here; but we've come to a halt in an old clearing—a former village site.

Only when Josh points them out do we notice house pits, shallow depressions in the ground. They once held single-room, sod-covered dwellings, dug in partway to insulate their inhabitants from high winds and wet cold.

Josh worked on an excavation here in 2002, as part of a joint project that involved students from both Alutiiq villages and the University of Alaska. With input from tribal governments and Native corporations, the Smithsonian's Arctic Studies Center designed a unique blend of oral history and archaeology research, combining it with outreach and education. Since the 1880s, no Alutiit have lived on the Kenai Peninsula's outer coast, but elders who foraged there seasonally until the 1950s visited the dig to reaffirm links with old homelands. One such tradition-bearer, a subsistence hunter and well-known kayak builder, helped to interpret findings at the site and thereby, to assess Aialik Bay's ability to support his ancestors.

In the context of Alutiiq sites in the park, which are close to 1,800 years old, Verdant Cove brings the past into sharper focus. Josh remembers that glass trade beads were unearthed here, and a pair of rusty shackles. The Smithsonian's archaeologists dated the settlement to around 1790, when Russian, British, and Spanish vessels made first contact along this coast.

The shackles across centuries darken the day, but the evidence is ambiguous. Were the Alutiit slaveholders or slaves, perpetrators or mere pawns in the Russian fur venture?

Both oral tradition and European written testimony recall Alutiiq headmen or family members kept hostage to coerce villagers into joining the sea otter-hunting fleets. Far from any oversight by imperial officials, *promyshlenniki* brutalized the population and levied tributes payable in pelts. They shanghaied women and men, taking them as far south as Fort Ross, a Russian American outpost in Alta California, where the captives tried to survive as company hunters, cooks, workers, or concubines. But the Alutiit in turn were not averse to bloodshed. They raided (and traded with) Yup'ik Eskimos, Aleuts, and Dena'ina Indians, taking slaves, or prisoners for ransom.

Overall though, they got the thick end of the cudgel.

By the mid-1800s, introduced diseases, indentured servitude, and starvation had reduced the Kodiak Islanders from 10,000 to 1,500. The Russians, after landing on Kodiak, repaid an act of Alutiiq resistance with musket and cannon fire. They cut down 300 women, children, and men who had fled to Refuge Rock on nearby Sitkalidak Island. "When our people revisited the place in the summer," the Alutiiq elder Arsenti Aminak remembered, "the stench of the corpses lying on the shore polluted the air so badly that none could stay there." The island has been uninhabited ever since.

Despite its tranquility, Verdant Cove betrays the dynamics of the outer coast to the observant visitor; like the reach of an empire, glaciers and earthquakes routinely disrupted landscapes and lives, fracturing the terrain.

There is more to be gleaned from these lonesome pits.

Middens at Verdant Cove and other nearby locations include

bones from harbor seals, sea lions, porpoises, cod, rockfish, and various seabirds. The Gulf of Alaska's cold, fertile upwelling offered a banquet for those who knew how to set the table. Consequently, on the Kenai coast, archaeological sites occupy every place where a kayak can land.

By the time sails flocked on Aialik's horizon and trade beads trickled into the villages, the sea and air in the Gulf had cooled significantly. The peak of a period commonly known as the Little Ice Age (1300 to 1850 CE) saw glaciers advancing to their most forward positions in recent times. Like earthquakes that dragged down stretches of coast, these glaciers depressed shorelines, even submerging some. Around the same time, epidemics scoured Alutiiq villages, sometimes ahead of the Russians. (Trade goods or middlemen could be carriers of smallpox and other diseases.) New illnesses, cannery jobs, climate change, or a combination of all three likely caused the late 19th-century abandonment of outer-coast villages that remains so vivid in Alutiiq memory.

Verdant Cove's belt of dead forest provides an eerie flashback but also a warning, a preview of more gradual but no less scary sea level rises from melting ice caps and glaciers. A largely ice-free, storm-driven sea already saps the Bering Strait village Shishmaref, forcing its residents to rebuild on higher ground. In addition to taking a physical beating, and perhaps more painfully, Alaska's coastal dwellers are losing faith in the knowledge and skills accumulated through the millennia. As hunters with snowmachines sink through weak ice into black waters, as sea creatures die off or ail, people no longer trust that which nourished them, the element that carried their ancestors' skin boats to landfall in a new world. One can only hope that once more their skills and resilience will let Native northerners steer true.

Today is a big day. We plan to round Aligo Point, the headland wedged between Aialik and Harris Bay. Because of the raw nature of the outer coast, only half of all Outward Bound kayaking courses make it into Northwestern Fjord on the far side. For beginners and even intermediate boaters to succeed, conditions need to be nearly perfect. Today they are. We launch early, with Gina leading the way. Chop causes the kayaks to corkscrew, and there is momentary confusion about certain landmarks, but we clear the cape without incident. After paddling up Granite Passage, helped by the incoming tide, we huddle briefly downwind of Granite Island. We are making excellent progress. Fire Cove, Ripple Cove, Crater Bay, Cataract Cove—each place brims with stories, stories we will not have time to learn on this trip.

Halfway up Harris Bay, combers in the main channel put us on edge. They break on the terminal moraine of Northwestern Glacier, now largely flooded at high tide. These shallows divide the bay from Northwestern Lagoon, barring large vessel traffic. We veer east and camp at Long Beach, where the sea took a bite out of Harris Peninsula, leaving a scimitar beach of fine gray sand. Its full sweep is impossible to capture, even on film: white peaks and granite scarps, clouds like Baroque wigs, rivulets leaping from snowfields above hanging gardens, sapphire curlers falling exhausted on shore.

The night brings rain, rain, rain, some wind, and more rain. Even our eggs, reconstituted from powder, are soggy this morning. After breakfast, Josh and I string out the students along the beach, widely spaced to ensure privacy for their twenty-four-hour solo, an Outward Bound tradition. Time alone with minimal distraction is meant to facilitate focus and perhaps realign goals while they're confined to small, individual tarp shelters. Because of the bears, they are not allowed to bring food. For many, solo is the most challenging part of a course.

Wind gusts kicking up whitecaps also dismantle some of the student tarps; but hardship is the currency of every Outward Bound trip. The investment almost always pays off. At the very least, this demonstrates why knots should be tied properly and tarps weighed down with driftwood. I hit the sack early, listening to the rain *pitter-patter* on my tent.

While we enact our program's traditions, the first people on this coast seek to revive some of theirs. The comeback of the *qayaq* is a good example. Worried that the lore and construction methods might fade together with their Native language, some elders have been initiating one more generation of boat-builders. They hope to pass on the essence of a sea-faring culture, to remind the world and their own children of a proud heritage.

Gregor Welpton, a Juneau shipwright and former commercial fisherman, apprenticed to the time-honored ways of building *qayat*. For Welpton, the conception of a boat's design, as well as its manufacture, are deeply spiritual and intuitive acts, ritualistic gestures pleasing the ancestors and the sea. "I hear it in my head," he says, "I feel it through my heart, it comes out through my hands and the boat is just completely born."

People who have paddled such replicas comment not only on their comfort, but also on the boat's translucence, the sensation of merging with their surroundings. Alutiiq elders who rode in a *qayaq*'s belly as children mention the light-and-shadow play on the hull and waves lapping like taps on a hand drum. Welpton compares this perfect communion, this best solitude on earth, to "slipping into the planet itself."

The low-pressure system has blown out overnight. Our soloists are happy to regroup, and we treat them to a big breakfast including an instant-mix cheesecake. Along with a cleansing wind, strong surf has come up. With five-foot breakers crashing onto the beach, we brief the group on surf launching. A small lagoon in the lee of a spit lets us sit in our kayaks and get prepared before heading out. I lead to demonstrate, synchronizing my strokes with the incoming waves to avoid a drubbing as they barrel down. From the "green zone," a calmer area offshore, I watch Chris, then Brett battle up and over steep seas. The heaving water dwarfs their kayaks, and I realize that the waves have grown too big and threatening.

We dallied too long breaking camp.

Josh signals from shore. He is out of his kayak, looking sheepish and wet. Avoiding the breakers' pull, I paddle close enough to hear him over the ruckus and learn that he got caught off guard and flipped—my turn to chuckle. He thinks we should abort the launch or at least look for a better place. With paddle signals, he coaches the students already afloat for their approach to the beach. The landings need to be quick and perfectly timed to the sea's rhythm. Bret hesitates to exit and pull up his kayak before the next punch arrives; he gets trapped in the seething backwash, broaches, and swims. Chris and I land smoothly as gulls on a storm-battered crag.

While we scout for another launch site, two sea lions play near shore. They mount the big rollers seemingly without effort and shoot down the opaque wave faces, sleek and shiny torpedoes. We are klutzes in our plastic shells next to these animals streamlined by currents and tides. For good measure, an explosive *harrumph* accentuates the waves' thumping. We scan the green zone, where a mist spout marks a humpback whale close by. It must be patrolling the estuary's nutritious outflow, which attracts salmon and smaller feeders. We watch it dive shallowly and surface repeatedly, each time with an aerosol puff. Arching its back and waving its fluke in glinting slow motion, it eventually sounds, headed for the open sea.

We find a place farther down the beach to push off the students one by one, timed to the wave sets. Giving the mid-bay shoals a wide berth we float above forests of bull kelp into quiet Northwestern Lagoon. Fish explode from the water around us; primed by the previous encounter and fooled by the grand scale of things, the mind mistakes their splashing for vapor from the blowholes of distant whales. Waves from our kayaks' bows fracture the light into myriads of facets, shattering mirror forests, glaciers, and fjords. Shedding gravity as if in an out-of-body experience, we soar through liquid space. Seesawing paddles flash in the sun like heliographs that signal *Bliss!* With each stroke, my boat rocks on its keel like a cradle, from starboard to port, and back. Push—pull—glide. Push—pull—glide.... I pause for split seconds between strokes to anticipate the water's resistance against my paddle blades and to better enjoy coasting. With my knees braced under the deck, I work my arms and upper body as levers of a well-oiled machine. Soon, the rhythm becomes hypnotic, and I enter "the zone" where ego dissolves and like the sea lions' play, movement is fluid, all-consuming purpose. The kayak has grown into an extension of my body, a means of ecstatic transport.

Not everybody reaches a trancelike state paddling. Our biggest student, Jake, rides in the double, as he has every day, because he feels unbalanced in a single and cramped in its smaller cockpit. Forced to synchronize his strokes as the back-man, he is focusing on his partner, which takes his mind off capsizing.

Unlike our assembly line kayaks, *qayat* were built to fit their owner like a foot does a buckskin boot. An Alutiiq hunter spent much of his life in such a boat—a hybrid being, part man and part dolphin—borne by and attuned to his environs. The bond between a man and his boat persisted even in death. Alutiiq hunters were typically buried with their kayaks, so they could ply the calm waters of afterlife.

The last two days are finals for the students. They get to run the show. It's their turn to demonstrate what they have learned, and Josh and I will intervene only if things become risky. The group wants to explore Northwestern Glacier, recessed deep into the head of the bay. Bleak, bare, and imposing, Striation Island guards the access, its granite flanks shot through with the quartzite veins that suggested its name. We look in vain for a place to land for a hike. As recently as the 1950s, the glacier held the island in an icy embrace, but since then has shrunk, like so many in Alaska and elsewhere. Our captain decides that the forbidding shore is unsafe and changes course. The navigators keep the pod close together and far enough from the fjord's walls to avoid chunks that could carom off a hanging glacier. We tack between jumbled facades from Redstone to Ogive to Anchor, each one resplendent alabaster and azure. At this point we have almost become inured to beauty, suffering sensory overload. Nearly two weeks' worth of scents, sounds, images, thoughts, and conversations swarms in our heads like schools of sparkling smelt. It will take months or longer for the students to fully absorb the experience. On some, it will have little impact. For others, it will be transformative, opening new perspectives, life choices. Some will never comprehend their role in all this. Others will follow invisible wakes and forever remember that the sea shifts in their bodies also.

Marooned

HE STUDENTS RECLINE in a half-circle in camp chairs facing the scalloped bay, afraid to miss out on the scenery. By week three of this thirty-day ed-venture, companionship, paddling skills, and new landscapes have begun to fill any void TV or video games may have left. Our surroundings help translate the course curriculum—politics and ecology of the Tongass National Forest—into realities that will become ingrained as memories. Luckily, no clear-cuts dissect today's view. In this part of Southeast Alaska's archipelago, hills dark with yellow cedar, hemlock, and Sitka spruce wrap around the bases of sudden massifs, part of the nation's largest public forest. Peaks throng above the tree line as do, higher still, barbed vanes of cirrus. Along the shore's scrawl, a dozen sea kayaks lie where we landed, beached like crayon-colored pilot whales. Gulls shriek in a winged blizzard near the high-water mark, pecking at dead things between the rocks. The tide carries notes of kelp, brine, mudflats, and decay—creation's inimitable perfume—while less than ten miles from us the hemisphere's southernmost tidal glacier dips its crystal tongue into the fjord. Mediterranean afternoons too rarely grace Alaska's Inside Passage; before we even pitch tents we take advantage of this one, teaching a lesson on glacial morphology. Lulled by the warmth and my co-instructor's voice, my concentration keeps slipping. A different, animal form of attentiveness takes over as I scan the beach for bears on the prowl.

Some bright, medium-sized creature *does* register in my field of vision, on an island afloat in the bay. Pacing from one end to the other, it appears to be testing the perimeter of its confinement. Could it be a wolf? I reach for my field glasses, tense enough to alert the group.

A head too small, and angular as slab marble, offsets a boulder-shaped body. Shag fluffs the creature's fore and hindquarters into ridiculous bloomers. A mountain goat. At sea level. The incoming tide has barred its retreat, stranding it like an ice chest washed off some tour boat or a bergy bit gone astray. At first glance it could be a billy or nanny. Both sexes sport jet-black spikes, which local Tlingit Indians carve into potlatch spoons—curved, functional keratin art. According to our guidebooks, adult male goats are the ones most likely to go gallivanting, from alpine reaches down crenellated ridges and into the shelter of conifers, lured by any ungulate tough guy's Shangri-la: salt licks, or deep meadows to browse and populate. Elusive as well as exclusive, the white ghost of the Coast Range was not described scientifically until 1900 and claims a genus all to itself. Earlier encounters with parts of its body had resulted in misunderstandings; on his journey along this ice-gouged, rugged littoral, Captain Cook traded for mountain goat hides, which he thought came from "spirit bears," the off-white black bear mutants of British Columbia's coast. (These bears are sacred, and the Natives would never have killed them.)

The students are standing now, firn lines and medial moraines temporarily consigned to their minds' garrets. Our intern, Neil, sprints to his kayak, slides into the cockpit, and, pushing with his knuckles, seal-launches from the beach.

"What are you going to do?" someone shouts. "Drape it across your bow?"

"Don't know," he replies. "Just taking a closer look, I guess."

Why not leave it be? I wonder. What feeds this need for proximity, this urge to interfere? "To cherish," Aldo Leopold mourned in *A Sand County Almanac*, "we must see and fondle, and when enough have seen and fondled, there is no wilderness left to cherish."

This "fondling" is not just a pat on the head. We nurse oil-slicked otters and eagles back to health. We radio-collar caribou to understand their timeless but timed rounds. We keep bears in cages, to edify, engage, enchant, entertain. We make room for wolves where we used to poison them and, just as absurdly, installed mountain goats in Nevada and Colorado, where trophy hunters can chase them. The sociobiologist E. O. Wilson claims that an attraction to other life forms took root in our genes when animals shaped hominid nature on Africa's steppes; hunter-gatherers acknowledge this debt with respect. Evolutionary psychologists also warn us that we neglect this relationship at the cost of societal dysfunction. To further complicate matters, this innate drive ("biophilia") can manifest as the opposite: a dark urge, born of greed or fear, to abuse and eradicate our brethren-on-Earth. Be they dachshunds or Komodo dragons, head lice or butterflies, cobras or Siamese cats, these others leave few people unmoved.

Regardless of its motivation, the reaching-out of a species that exiled itself behind barriers of artifice can be a bleak and beautiful thing. I only hope nobody will suffer injury or indignity on this occasion. While Neil disembarks on the low-slung island, the goat gallops up and over a rise. Neil walks to the top, neoprene skirted, paddle in hand, to see what we have already seen from shore: the goat churning toward an outcrop close by, muzzle pointed skyward, cutting a wake like a chunky retriever.

By the time Neil has inserted himself in the kayak again, the billy has climbed this miniature Ararat doomed to submerge. Against the sea's backdrop, the animal seems out of its element but still more of this place than we Gore-Tex-clad visitors from afar. Possessed of a mineral quality, a poise and resilience older than flesh, it stands riveted to rock—an extension of sweeping summits, hewn from Le Conte Glacier's trunk, hefty and blunt as winter itself. Its stubborn form embodies the land's pluck and fiber. Like snowfields crisp in the distance or the void on explorers' charts, the goat not only invites speculation but even more so the projection of desires. I would trade with this bearded recluse in an instant. I'd travel unburdened by gear. I'd grow hairy and hunchbacked and rank, sniffing mates and competitors. I'd become agile enough to dodge grizzlies and wolves, fearless enough to bed down on vertiginous ledges, and smart enough to avoid our kind.

With a lapse into pastoral metaphor excusable in a Scotsman, wilderness sage John Muir compared this breed to others, considering them, "nature's cattle," better fed and protected from the cold. But he also acknowledged the grit in their existence. During a sledding trip above Glacier Bay, on the ice flow that still bears his name, he found bones cast about in an ancient blood ritual. Their configuration spelled out the death of a frail or sick or unlucky one. Presumably, wolves had caught up with a wild goat two miles from safer ground, where breakneck terrain matched with ballerina grace would have given it the advantage. Despite their famed surefootedness, missteps occur, and the abyss claims its share of mountain goats every year. Loose rocks and avalanches strike down others. Inexperienced kid goats may fall to the talons of golden eagles, which hunt alone or pair up to corner them. Current logging practices in the Tongass, stripping its slopes of cover and feed, further skew the odds against survival in the margins.

Pulling away from those sobering thoughts, I watch Neil bump the outcrop with the bow of his kayak. He waves a paddle blade in the animal's face. What is he doing? Trying to save a goat by making it dive? It's unlikely to drown, even if it gets flooded out. But Neil might yet discover the flip side of hands-on approaches to learning. If the goat chooses to answer intrusion with uncivil disobedience, our rookie instructor will have a hard time explaining hoof scratches on his kayak deck back at the warehouse.

Clearly annoyed with being crowded, the billy indeed takes him on, defending its quickly shrinking domain. It jerks horn daggers into Neil's direction, hooking the air, unwilling to yield as much as an inch.

On shore, the students holler and cheer—for whom, I cannot tell.

Eventually, the goat's aversion to humans overcomes any fear of the unfamiliar. (It knows nothing about tiderips, reefs, or orcas). With shoulders tucked in like a boxer's, it pivots and leaps high and wide, charging its twin in the burnished sea. Before long we lose sight of it as it churns across the bay, into Muir's "endless combinations of water and land," to be culled from the gene pool or to sire a feisty clan somewhere in the high country.

Tough Times on Denali

W HY CLIMB EVEREST? Because it's there, British moun-
taineer George Leigh Mallory allegedly told a reporter
before his 1921 attempt to attain the highest point on earth. He
post-holed into the twilight of history on his third try, in 1924,
joining the pantheon of Alpinist gods. His remains were only
discovered sixteen years ago, and there is still doubt whether
or not he was the first to summit Mount Everest. Why indeed
climb any mountain? Why breathe? Why love? Why speculate
about the meaning of life? The answer: we cannot help it. It is
part of our nature.

Why did I want to climb Denali? Because it teased me each
clear-enough day, as I biked to the campus library above Fairbanks and the Chena River floodplain. Because it just hovered
there on the horizon, splendidly remote, a cool and ethereal
presence boasting immaculate symmetry. Because it seemed
unreachable and in its aloofness perfectly captured the Great
Land's spirit. I did not want to take this peak's measure because

of its height or to break any records but simply to escape gravity, to cast off into the oceanic blue that engulfs its bold crest.

A chance to scale Denali came sooner than expected. Laurent Dick, a friend who lived outside of town, was planning his first ascent. Laurent had grown up with mountains, but his birthplace, Switzerland, had become stifling, and he sought purer air and less tainted landscapes elsewhere. When we first met, he was a student of photojournalism with a yen for nature photography, striving, like myself, to wring a living from his passions.

Everybody whom Laurent asked to come along had prior commitments; but solo climbs on Denali are considered slightly suicidal. And so, I was on. Even with two people, the margin of safety was slim. Except for Mont Blanc in the French Alps and an attempt on Mexico's Popocatepetl cut short by nosebleeds and viselike headaches, my mountaineering resume was less than impressive. I had never topped 16,000 feet or endured the rigors of Arctic cold fronts. I did not know how well I would handle the lack of oxygen or symptoms of mountain sickness at an elevation of 20,300 feet.

After the invitation had been issued, I started to borrow gear. My neighbor loaned me skis, a pair of crampons, and his *pulk*, a Scandinavian-style plastic sled with harness to which I would hitch myself to pull part of our load. My outfit represented a strange mix of Aspen and bush Alaska: plastic ski boots, Polartec fleece, and Gore-Tex pants combined with a fur-ruffed down parka and beaver skin hat. (There are certain things modern technology simply cannot improve.)

We fretted over gear and food lists, adding or subtracting items according to advice from Denali veterans or our current readings. I was preparing mentally with an account of the first *winter solo* ascent, cozily titled *Minus 148 Degrees*. When we finally loaded the truck, the amount of gear and provisions we'd be carrying more than two miles up vertical wasteland struck me as fit for a mule. I thought I was in decent shape, having schlepped food, tents, rifles, and bears' skins and their skulls for trophy hunters through Kodiak Island all April.

Bad luck swooped down on us right away. Cracking walnuts on the ride south, I broke a filling in one of my canines. A short stop at the Healy gas station where I bought Super Glue took care of the problem.

In Talkeetna, we checked in with the National Park Service for our mandatory briefing and to hand over our fee for recreating on public lands. A few last-minute purchases at the local sporting goods store, and we were on our way.

Our pilot was Jay Hudson, owner of a family business that had been shuttling the curious and ambitious to and from the mountain for half a century. His wheel-and-ski-equipped Cessna quickly gained altitude, leaving behind the ramshackle town that resembled a child's carelessly tossed wooden building blocks. The Susitna River glinted between gray gravel bars; cloud shadows undulated across the land, lending it texture and contrast. Soon, green foothills yielded to the monastic hues of the Alaska Range. Jay aimed straight for the V notch in a rampart of minor peaks; this was One Shot Pass, the shortest and most direct route to Base Camp at 7,200 feet on the southeast fork of Kahiltna Glacier. Buffeted by tailwinds or downdrafts, and often trapped under a low cloud ceiling, pilots have to get their line right the first time. When Jay aligned our Cessna with Kahiltna's crevasse field, the pass framed the plane like a gun sight—its wingtips appeared to be grazing precipitous snowfields and avalanche chutes on both sides. Ahead of us, as the glacier's backdrop, Mt. Foraker and Mt. Hunter flanked the Great One. Perceiving the world as a maze of relationships, the region's Athabaskan inhabitants thought of the two subaltern peaks as Denali's wife and child.

As soon as the propeller sputtered to a standstill, Jay unlatched the door and we started to pile gear into the snow. In less than fifteen minutes, we had the plane unloaded. It taxied back to the improvised airstrip of compacted snow, dusting us in a wake of spindrift. As the Cessna took off, its drone boomeranged off cirques and arêtes.

Laurent had warned me not to expect solitude on this venture. But I was still unprepared for the bustle at "Kahiltna International"—up to 100 women and men at a time occupied this outpost. Denali's gateway was a makeshift encampment, a tent city fortified against the whims of the weather. It replicated frontier society, Babel transposed to the North. Flags of different nations snapped in the breeze; gear sprawled everywhere, and people hobnobbed or reclined in lawn chairs in front of their compounds. Austrians joked with Canadians. Italians drank wine with Kiwis and Japanese. Koreans talked routes with Argentineans, Poles, and even a few Chinese. Unfamiliar accents and languages mingled with cooking scents. Some residents had built elaborate snow kitchens, complete with benches and shelves. Climbers waited in line at the entrance to the outhouse, a euphemism, really, for a portable toilet half-sunk into a snow pit. Tax dollars had paid for it, and the National Park Service airlifted it to Talkeetna regularly to be cleaned. I figured it was the most scenic "bathroom" in North America. But, wind or no wind, you certainly would not linger over the view. Everywhere, people coiled ropes, adjusted crampons, or sorted provisions. Bamboo wands tipped with orange flags marked food caches in the snow.

The runway hummed with activity as more planes landed and took off. Despite the chaos, a sense of purpose and urgency galvanized the crowd, like an army preparing to lay siege to a hill fort.

The characters you run into on the mountain are a big part of the experience. Some couples climbed Denali for their honeymoon. Bald-headed Vern Tejas, who played fiddle on summits, had first winter-soloed Denali, and would go on to scale the highest peak on each continent at a record age of fifty-seven, was rumored to be around. And one of the rangers at the 14,200-foot camp had been a rodeo clown in a previous life. He was still saving people's skins, but now in a much bigger and colder arena. On a whim, he had once circumnavigated the Great One on skis, in the middle of winter. The Talkeetna flyboys, too, were chips from a different block. Doug Geeting, who used to tow advertising banners high above oiled flesh roasting on California's beaches, was not only one of the most daring pilots around but also a writer and award-winning folk musician.

After we'd dug out a level foundation and set up our tent, Laurent checked in with the base camp manager. Annie Duquette lived on site for the entire season, in a Weatherport, a rigid shelter scarcely more comfortable than a tent. She acted as air traffic controller, Park Service liaison, shrink, nurse and mother figure, and source of information about weather and climbing conditions. The woman the climbing rangers called an icon did pull-ups from a bar installed in her hut when things were slow. On call twenty-four hours a day, "Base Camp Annie" made sure things ran smoothly in this off-kilter microcosm representative of what is commonly though erroneously called "the real world," a built world of shallow time.

I only found leisure to fully take in my environs after we had settled in. Mount Hunter's face soared more than a mile above the Kahiltna, at an angle close to forty degrees. Since we arrived, already two avalanches had scoured its face: billowing, thunderous slides, smothering crystal-breath death that raced halfway across the glacier. It had taken the snow clouds minutes to settle. Each time the mountain let go, camp business ceased and all attention centered on the spectacle.

In the calm in-between, I was comfortable enough to lounge about in our flat wearing only a T-shirt. Laurent visited neighbors, gathering news about conditions higher up; but I did not want to meet people just yet, absorbing the warmth and time by myself. The camp stove roared along merrily as I kept feeding the cooking pot snow. This was the only source of water around, and we'd fired up as soon as our tent was pitched. With the devotion of monks we would melt snow for several hours every day, because dry air and exertion sapped our bodies' fluids.

A late sun pinked Mount Foraker's spine, while silver-lined clouds hooded Denali's crown. The scale of things made it hard to judge distances. I knew it was eight miles from our camp to the summit, but straight lines were impossibilities in this terrain. The enormity of our endeavor was corroding my confidence. Perhaps we did not belong there. Indigenous people who always had shunned the mountain understood this; human bodies and minds were not designed for such hostile environments. Overwhelmed by sensations, I curled up in my down sleeping bag early, deciding to take one step at a time.

The next two weeks passed in a blur of snow, insomnia, and oxygen deprivation. Eventually, the monotony of movement numbed all thought; our bodies shrank into nothing but focused breathing, our minds into tight fists. Eventually, even the pain evaporated. We lived like ticks in dog fur, entrenched in the glacier's skin, not for nourishment but for protection. At 16,200 feet, Laurent showed signs of altitude sickness, and we had to descend again. Next we sat two days stormbound in our tent, which whopped like a helicopter, so loud that we couldn't talk. Running out of reading material, we studied the prescription drug pamphlets in our first aid kit. I suffered an abscessed tooth (not the canine), flushed to the gills with painkillers and antibiotics from the rangers' med tent. (The doc on duty had served as a dentist on Himalayan expeditions.) We finally summited, owing our success to stubbornness and extra fuel and food rather than to good sense. The view from the top, though, scrolled out with more detail than a map, made each minute worthwhile. Becalmed by the occasional basin, lesser peaks of the Alaska Range broke on Denali's escarpment like surf frozen in mid-motion. Glaciers scaly and wrinkled with age scraped their way through the massif's heart. Clouds ballooned, tethered to a horizon that from our vantage appeared to be visibly curving. If the crampons' bite had not grounded me I would have floated off into deep, blue-black outer space.

On our descent, the Football Field, the Archdeacon's Tower, Denali Pass, High Camp, the Buttress, the Headwall, Basin Camp, Windy Corner, and Motorcycle Hill passed by, dreamlike and without incident. At 11,000 feet we switched from crampons back to the skis and *pulks* we had cached there, faced downhill and let fly. After days of hauling loads and moving like zombies, the burst of speed brought on head rushes. We kicked up white rooster tails, flashed past strings of climbers who still trudged up the mountain. With the recklessness of people in need of beer and a cleanup, we zipped across narrow snow bridges softening under the June sun. In tricky places I flipped my *pulk* upside-down, and it slowed me like a dragging anchor.

Before we reached the base camp on the Kahiltna, we slogged up a hump whose name had amused us on the day we set out. Returning, it made sudden sense: Heartbreak Hill. It could have been called "Just when you thought you made it...."

Foul weather was upon us once again. Steeped in fog thick enough to spoon, the camp brought to mind an underworld populated by shadows. Half-buried tents clustered together as if seeking company and the maze of trails and embankments looked unfamiliar in the white expanse. Fluff fell from the ripped bellies of clouds. Rope teams were abandoning the mountain, eager to head out for the solstice bash at Talkeetna's historic Fairview Inn. But in this weather not even Alaska bush pilots dared to fly. Glued to Annie's radio, we waited for updates. We visited, we bragged, we compared gear, exchanged addresses, and dug up and shared supplies the marauding ravens had overlooked.

Halfway through the morning, a pale sun elbowed its way in, and baby-blue gaps showed in the scrim. Almost immediately, overdue planes started buzzing in; the ensuing commotion resembled the rush to the lifeboats aboard *Titanic*. Climbers scurried about, shuttling gear to the runway—except that three feet of fresh snow cushioned the ground where the runway used to be. More levelheaded or seasoned mountaineers assisted the pilots by stomping out a landing strip with snowshoes and skis in a klutzy square dance. Some planes briefly touched down in mock landings to compress the snow. One unfortunate soul veered into drifts, where his Cessna bogged down. Another flipped, but was lucky enough to crawl from the wreck unharmed. (With the help of a steel cable, a chopper later airlifted the mess to Talkeetna.) A few of us pushed stuck planes by their wing struts, blasted with whiteout from the engines, needled by propeller-whipped snow.

After repeated sorties to the glacier's deck and shuttles to town, our bird dropped from the sky once again. We boarded in a hurry. A last peek through the Cessna's scratched Plexiglas panes showed the focus of our desire falling away. From up high, base camp looked abstract and lifeless, a diorama or blue Delft tile already fading into a memory.

At the Talkeetna airfield, Laurent and I gulped down balmy air, staring in disbelief at a world that wallowed in tender greens around the parked Cessna.

Having stuffed our faces with real food—pizza and salad at the McKinley Deli—we ambled to the bunkhouse for a shower. A glance at the half-blind mirror convinced me that I'd lost ten years and about twenty pounds on the mountain. We relished water hot enough to raise welts before charging the historic Fairview Inn like polar explorers would have a mirage. But wonder of wonders, this haven did not dissolve. I opened its hefty door to find the place packed, though it was only four in the afternoon. For a minute, I just stood immersed in cigarette smoke and warm humanity, flabbergasted by the den atmosphere. The current of voices, the clinking of bottles and glasses overlaid with women's laughter, the bellowing of climbers glad to be alive, belied the mountain's composure. Climbers outnumbered the locals, both working hard on hydration. You could tell who was outbound from who'd just returned. The latter looked burnt, raw, reduced, somehow, to an essence. I tried to read failure or success in the lined faces. Regardless of outcome, Denali had honed edges in everyone, edges that cut into new and lasting truths.

The rounds kept coming, and I didn't know who was buying. By the time dusk, or what passes for it on summer solstice in these latitudes, dimmed the windows, our waitresses had kicked off their shoes and no longer ran tabs. As the home planet wobbled precariously on its axis, spinning, and racing back toward winter, I became nauseous. Before I left, I caught sight of Laurent atop the bar. Weaving like a bamboo wand in a gale, he was planting a miniature Swiss flag on the summit of an oil painting of Denali, and having a tough time with it. But till dawn at least, for him and for others in there, wild abandon would cloak the sight, lodged firmly as ice screws, of a body laid out in a black rubber cocoon at 14,200 feet.

Mating Dance under the Midnight Sun

With each paddle stroke, muscles play in her tanned, well-rounded shoulders. Straight, chestnut-colored hair falls to the nape of her neck, barely concealing the swan-like curve.

"Such a beautiful day, *non*?"

It is indeed. I cannot believe my luck. Here I am, with an exotic woman, on a remote northern river, a blue sky smiling above everything.

What more could a man want?

It all began with an ad. Or rather, with the idea that, after so many years of romantic shipwrecks, of forever stumbling into the pits of physical attraction and carnal confusion, a soul mate could perhaps better be found by comparing souls.

I therefore decided to have my profile printed in *Alaska Men* magazine, the path-breaking periodical that has been "bringing you Alaska bachelors since 1987." "You," meaning the female half of the Lower Forty-Eight states. "Bachelors," meaning, "husband material," in the words of the magazine editor herself. This illustrious and illustrated gem also gave the world a T-shirt with the slogan *Alaska Men—The odds are good, but the goods are odd* and the Firefighter Calendar, a long-overdue male equivalent of the swimsuit calendar and Playboy centerfold. Actually, the odds in places like Fairbanks or Anchorage seem about even, and as for oddity—judge for yourself. I certainly qualified for the honorific Alaska Man. Although German-born, I had been a resident of the Big Dipper State for almost four years.

So, undaunted by the commodification of my body, I sent in a filled-out questionnaire, together with a picture of my expressive, clean-cut features against the backdrop of a bush plane. (Not my own—the plane, that is.) Asked to describe my ideal first date to the readers, I did not hesitate for a second: *My ideal first date would be a weeklong wilderness trip together, because I believe that's where your compatibility and true colors show quickly.* They ran a full page in the magazine, and I was happy with the way I looked and sounded on glossy paper.

I was hoping for the mother lode this time around.

As a safety precaution against love-crazed stalkers, crank calls or bomb threats from jealous exes or current boyfriends, I had my phone number unlisted and rented a mailbox at the post office in town. (*Paranoid* was not one of the character traits I had cared to mention in my sales pitch.) As it turned out, the readership was rather diverse and not at all limited to the continental United States. I received fan mail from England. One letter arrived from Quebec, in broken English, another from a black nurse in Kotzebue. A lonely-sounding fisherwoman trawling off the coast of South Africa cast her net wide and wrote to me on yellow legal-pad paper. One of my female pen pals grew up in a lighthouse. She admitted she talked a lot with dead people. I received notes from prison inmates that made me blush, although I pride myself on not being prudish. Some epistles contained locks of hair. Others were smudged with lipstick kisses, or steeped in mysterious perfumes.

Quite a few women were suspicious. They wanted to know why I had used a portrait shot for a photo. Was I obese, or missing a limb? Foolishly, I had believed in the old saw that eyes are the windows to the soul. I quickly became an expert graphologist, a reader-between-lines. Occasionally, the colorful stamps intrigued more than the enclosed words. But every time I peered into the dark innards of my mailbox and spotted the white or pink flash of envelopes, I trembled with the prospect of having hit the jackpot. Letters and pictures of women in various poses and stages of life lay scattered all over my fourteen-by-fourteen-foot plywood palace without running water. (Hence the self-described *rustic minimalist* in the magazine.) I bought a cardboard folder and organized my correspondence alphabetically and felt like a little boy locked into the candy store overnight.

A flurry of letter writing ensued with a few fortunate candidates. And bit-by-bit, as I got to meet their souls, and they mine, the choice became clear.

Monique was a French woman living in Albuquerque, a lover of literature and a painter. I personally prefer Edward Abbey's rants to Simone de Beauvoir, and much of photographic realism strikes me as uninspired. But I felt I had to make some concessions. Monique had divorced her husband, a former salvage diver, when he turned into a couch potato. My kind of woman exactly. As I could not make out her soul's apertures in the diminutive photo she'd sent, I asked for an enlargement. The watercolor self-portrait that promptly arrived in the mail showed nothing but a pair of hazel cat's eyes afloat on lush paper. Long lashes, and brows arched like calligraphy brush strokes sent harpoons straight into my chest. Perhaps too soon, we swapped phone numbers; but the first time her sweet, melodious lilt bridged the distance between us I could have gobbled up the receiver.

When she finally walked through the gate at the Fairbanks airport, my heart danced a little jig. She looked like a French version of Audrey Hepburn. Except, with her delicate five-foot-four frame, she was shorter than I expected—about half the size of the glass-encased grizzly bear by the Alaska Airlines counter. Monique had told me her height, but it had never quite registered, and I am bad with numbers anyway. (In my self-portrait, that translated into *concerned with quality rather than quantity*.)

She knew, however, that the way into the heart of a Taurus is through his belly. In my modest kitchen nook, she went straight to work, preparing a dish of braised scallops, green asparagus, potatoes au gratin, smothered in a killer sauce of heavy cream and Cognac (no cheap brandy for her), something with a nasal-sounding name I can't quite remember. That first night, we slept chastely apart, myself in the stuffy loft reached via ladder and hatch and Monique on the floor of my domicile, which tilts slightly, because I live on permafrost in the muskeg around town.

On our first full day together, we did touristy things. Aboard the sternwheeler *Discovery* we plowed the silty flood of the Chena River, while the theme music of *Love Boat* played in my head. We stopped at Susan Butcher's place, and the famous musher welcomed us from her backyard. Leaning on the rails of the big white riverboat, we watched Susan's handler race her Iditarod-winning team. The huskies looked a little hot on this subarctic summer day, as they pulled a sled around the yard, their driver barely visible behind dust clouds.

"But there is no snow," observed my lovely companion.

"We Alaskans do things differently," I reassured her.

We spent a pleasant-enough evening at the Malemute Saloon of the old Ester Gold Camp. Monique got her first glimpse of

Alaskan manhood and mores from the upright-piano player, a token Sourdough dressed in nineteenth-century garb, who kept spitting with great relish into the sawdust that covered the floor.

During my weekly soccer game Monique sat at the sidelines. Our team was "Buns on the Run," and our sponsor, a fast-food breakfast place, had donated shorts too tight, with the business name scrawled on their backsides. Instead of watching the odd goods milling about on the ball field, Monique chatted with the wives and fiancées of my teammates. While I appreciated having a trained nurse in attendance—we were losing, and things were getting a bit rough—a shadow of domesticity fell onto my soul. I imagined that scene as a replay of my Mom watching my Dad kick a pig's bladder around some Hessian cow pasture, thirty-two years ago. It had happened that way. I had happened that way.

The day after, a small plane delivered us to the banks of the Koyukuk River, north of the Arctic Circle, where its turbid flow skirts the village of Allakaket. Our great adventure was about to begin.

Between piles of gear, I wrestled with the Klepper, the collapsible double kayak made-in-the-old-country that was to be our craft. I remembered that the brand name is a Teutonic term for a nag ready to be sent to the knacker. Out of their packsack, the canvas deck and rubberized bottom, the keel, ribs, thwarts, gunwales and rudder parts, more closely resembled the remains of a seal butchered on shore. I could not make sense of the gibberish German instructions, even though I was still fluent in that language. (*Manually challenged* was another trait that never made it into print, because it clashed with *self-reliant* and *down-to-earth*.) With the help of my fine-boned visitor from the high desert and advice from a number of Indian spectators, I eventually figured out where all the *Flügelmuttern* and *Kreuzschlitzschrauben* needed to go. We assembled The Thing and shoved off.

"Should we look for a camp, Mai-kel?" Monique now warbles from the bow of the boat.

I just love the way she pronounces my name.

"*Biensure*," I flaunt my command of the Gallic tongue and contemplate adding a "*cherie*" for good measure.

We make camp in a clearing overlooking the river. Humping the contents of our craft up the steep bank, I realize I forgot a minor piece of equipment—the cooking pot. (It was all there, out in the open, black on white in *Alaska Men*: . . . *not obsessing about the mundane details of life. . . .*) I prove my resourcefulness and worth as a paramour by emptying the can of Coleman fuel for the stove into our water bottles. We will have to dip drinking water with our cups straight from the river. So what, a little sediment never hurt anybody. With the saw of my Leatherman, I then cut the one-gallon tin can in half. The upper part, hammered flat with a rock, makes a nice lid, the bottom a beautiful, if sharp-lipped, pot.

"Voila!" I beam.

I can see admiration in Monique's eyes, and her radiant smile reveals a chipped front tooth cute enough to die for. My knees feel like the green Jell-O I keep hidden as a surprise dessert. Our pasta-and-tomato-sauce dinner is slightly compromised by an aftertaste of gasoline, which, I feel confident, will be gone in a day or two. And anyway, this is robust bush fare, not some kind of city cuisine.

After we have cleaned dishes in a low-impact style, with gravel and sand, we set up our shelter. I left the roomy three-person dome tent at home and brought the doghouse instead. We are comfy inside, lying on top of an unzipped sleeping bag— a shared sleeping bag!

"Tell me about your life in Alaska," she demands.

Great, I think, time for some pillow talk, and proceed to recount the adventures of the spring I was working for big game hunting outfits on Kodiak Island and near Katmai's volcanoes.

"I hauled supplies from sea level up into the mountains, and forty-pound bearskins and skulls back to the boats. It was the perfect preparation for an ascent of Denali the following summer." I can tell she is impressed when she snuggles closer. I go on to recount an episode in Glacier Bay National Park, failing to mention that I flew there to meet another blind date. (She turned out to be—but that's a different story.)

"I was out sea-kayaking, trying to get close to a griz on a spit of land, to get a better picture of him. Next thing you know, he jumps into the drink and starts dogpaddling after me."

The instant these words come out of my mouth, I realize they were a mistake.

"There are bears out here too, *n'est que pas*?" Her voice almost falters.

"Sure—I don't know, actually." What else is there to say?

"Ssssh! What was that?"

"What?"

"That sound. Like a splash.

"Probably just a piece of cutbank slumping into the river."

"No, lis-ten!"

And we both do, and her body is rigid, and I can sense tension coming off her like heat. The economy-size can of bear repellent lying handily at the foot of our love nest probably does not help much to alleviate her fear. I stay quiet, but all I can hear before drifting into sleep is an ominous rumbling in the distance.

Before long the midsummer sun tilts upward on its low arc and light caresses the tops of black spruce trees on a bluff, which resemble big bottlebrushes. I walk to the morning-still river, urged by my bladder. Mocha-colored water roils at the tip of my boots. Something about its hue strikes me as odd. Scanning the beach, I cannot see our paddles.

"Monique."

"Yes?" comes her voice from the tent, still heavy with sleep.

"Did you put the kayak paddles away last night?"

"No. *Pourquoi?*"

"They must be here, somewhere."

I look inside the boat, behind the tent, behind bushes. Nothing. Suddenly the truth hits me in hot and cold flashes. The river has come up. It must have been raining hard last night and only upstream. Unloading the boat, I had simply dropped the damned wooden paddles and, like a cheechako, left them lying on the beach. The flood took them away.

"*Merde alors!*" Monique's words, not mine. She is wrapped in her sleeping bag, her sculpted collarbones exposed to the new day, which all of a sudden promises to be bleak.

I just stand there, *six feet tall, blond, blue-eyed, confident and comfortable in the outdoors*, God's gift to womanhood.

After a quick and tense breakfast, we are back on the water. I guess we could line the kayak downstream, following the brush fringe of the Koyukuk, but I decide to forego a bushwhacking ordeal. Not easily browbeaten by the weather's antics, we pole downriver instead, using unwieldy lengths of driftwood. This is very awkward from a sitting position, and the poles only help with propulsion where the river is shallow enough. When I try it kneeling, the kayak threatens to capsize. The current is sluggish; at this pace it could take us weeks to get to Hughes.

The next few days are best forgotten. They stretch before us endlessly, an impression that can only in part be credited to the untiring Arctic sun.

The poles break frequently and need to be replaced. When they do, the Klepper truly behaves like a horse carcass. It turns sideways, grinds into gravel bars, or helplessly drifts toward dangerous strainers—fallen trees skimming the surface. They vibrate in the stream's passing, potential deathtraps with the power to pin and flip boats, to keep swimmers' heads underwater. Whenever Monique lowers herself to looking at me, I can see deep lines furrowing her once-comely brow. At some point I try to cheer her up.

"This could be Venice, and I could be your *gondoliere*." (Did I mention *great sense of humor?*) More frosty frowns are my only reward, and I wonder if it could be a cultural thing. Perhaps the French don't like the Italians.

In the evenings I lie in my sleeping bag by myself, with sore shoulders and blistered hands, too tired and raw to even think about touching this attractive woman next to me. Instead, I calculate food rations and distances in my head.

Six days out, we pitch the tent on a half-moon of gravel on the inside curve of a river meander. By now, I wear boxing gloves made of bandages from the First Aid kit. Nevertheless, tonight is the night. Tonight, I will make my move. Tonight, I will check my soul mate's compatibility. During dinner, Monique had talked to me again, even laughed at some half-hearted jokes. (I had served her pea soup "au cretin," with a flourish: a filthy bandana draped over my arm.) I start by removing the wraps around my fists, flexing stiff joints. This will be bare-knuckles. Last man standing.

Just as I roll over, crunching footfalls draw close to the tent. They stop abruptly. Silence. In one fluid move I reach for the bear spray, roll out of the sleeping bag and poke my head through the tent flap (...*athletic*...). I am determined to protect this babe in the woods, if necessary, at the cost of my life.

"Hi, guys. This is tribal land. Part of the village of Hughes."

"Why? How close are we?" I ask the young man with slightly Asiatic features, who waits respectfully ten feet from the tent.

"'Bout half a mile."

"I had no idea we were that close," I apologize. Knowing that the river would get us where we needed to go, I had not brought maps either.

"There is a camping fee, if you guys spend the night here."

I look for my wallet, which I *did* bring. You never know, even the bush is getting expensive these days. I pay, our Koyukon host nods, and leaves. Back inside I realize the spark of desire has been snuffed out. It could have been the interruption, but more likely, forking out fifteen bucks for a campsite without showers, picnic tables, or even a barbecue pit, has cooled my ardor.

Next morning, we land at the village. Skilled hunters who have steered small watercraft for thousands of years are gathered on the riverbank to observe our deft maneuvering. Word must have gone out or else they saw us coming. On the improvised boat slip, I busy myself with the load, trying to avoid eye contact with the elders. With their broad, leathery faces, their quiet poise and demeanor, these are true Alaska men, the genuine article.

"You know, they make real nice kickers now," one of them volunteers.

"I know. Goddamn paddles, too," I curse under my breath.

Back in Fairbanks, we are saying our good-byes at the airport. "Will you call me when you get to Albuquerque?" "Perhaps." A quick hug, a peck on both cheeks that makes me feel like a European head of state, and Audrey Hepburn disappears through the gate, a figment of my inflammation.

One week later Monique called from Albuquerque, admitting she had a six-year-old boy and never intended to move to Alaska.

As soon as I found out, I built a bonfire and torched my file of letters in the yard, *given to histrionics*. From the bench on my rickety porch, I watched fat flakes of ash rise above tangles of fireweed that was already beginning to turn. I contemplated the odds of another long winter holed up in my cabin. Baking twelve kinds of Christmas cookies for myself. Probably talking to the ravens again, by March at the latest. To hell with it! I sighed and fed my complimentary copy of *Alaska Men* to the flames.

Biking Cool

E ACH FALL I COMPILE A TO-DO LIST for winterizing my bike, hoping to get around to these things before first flurries of "termination dust" make tinkering outside undesirable. *Slightly deflate tires for better traction on snow.* (No money to buy studded ones.) *Put on low-temperature chain grease.* (Makes riding in low gears actually feel like riding in low gears.) *Dig "poagies"—mitten-like insulated shells—from piles in storage trailer and attach to handlebars.* (They help you keep fingers, which are useful for shifting gears.) *Add various reflectors and change batteries in headlamp.* (December nights in Fairbanks last sixteen hours, and not even the gaudiest blowing-curtain auroras give off enough light to navigate by.) The local high-end sporting goods store advertises a Cold Weather Clinic for bikers. But, except for its clanking ball bearings and wobbly pedals, my trusted steel mule seems to be doing fine.

Needless to say, each fall I step outside my cabin some morning to find snow piled on the seat of my still unmodified ride. I *did* compromise my vision of a small-town home by relocating to Fairbanks, Alaska's second-largest city, because my girlfriend found work here. But living a few miles from town—without running water, at least until spring melts the snow on the cabin roof—definitely feels rural. It keeps face-to-face interactions with people limited and meaningful. As for the biking—even a cursory survey of trials and tribulations shows that riding the wintry urban range equals the best Moab's slickrock can offer.

This is no place for tight spandex outfits that cost as much as a custom-tailored tux; heavy wool army pants, baggy enough for two pairs of long underwear, will keep vital parts functioning. Footwear consists of knee-high, homemade nylon-shell mukluks with felt liners. A hooded down parka, beaver-skin hat (preferably with ear flaps), and fleece mittens complete the outfit. A full beard or balaclava comes in handy on breezy days and keeps subarctic cold from peeling your face. (But I take off the mask when entering banks or convenience stores.) Because of the cushioning effect of these garments, wearing knee and elbow pads is unnecessary, unsightly, if not impossible. Helmets don't fit over Soviet-style fur hats, and the only chance for abrasions is doing a facedown on salted roads.

Allow ample time for dressing and undressing.

Much gear is field-tested for suitability and adapted accordingly. During my first winter of riding at forty below, I wore a sweater with a metal zipper. Had I remembered that metal is an excellent conductor, I could easily have avoided the nickel-sized frost blister on my Adam's apple. On a different day, my tongue stuck to the bike's padlock, which I tried thawing out with my breath. In short, while desert bikers worry about dehydration or sunburn, their taiga counterparts have to work hard to keep their noses from falling off.

Another hazard, surprisingly, is air quality. While Moab may taunt you with dust squalls or headwinds, "ice fog" is the boreal biker's bane. It's suspended, freezing moisture mixed with the reek from too many households burning green wood and from cars left idling because they likely will not restart. (Rumors that your lungs will freeze to your rib cage are just that—a tall tale for scaring tenderfeet.) Even on clear days, deeply inhaled cold and dry air burns in your windpipe and bronchial tubes. In the summertime, the chokehold of wildfires that consume the state can make you hack like a consumptive. It's as much fun as having your respiratory system sandpapered.

Rather than landing jumps or doing wheelies, my great feat of balance is staying upright on two wheels on level ground. "Black ice" forms near traffic lights and intersections where car exhaust briefly melts snow that refreezes. I've learned to avoid rash braking and steering maneuvers, and have perfected the paratrooper shoulder roll. Although I am not skirting sheer drops like those along Moab's Portal trail, I have found opportunities to practice equilibrium. I once parked my bike outside the supermarket in town only to find a thief had lifted my quick-release seat. With a backpack full of groceries, I pedaled five miles standing up. (Nobody has enough bottom padding to sit on *that*.) Steering one-handed between the snowplowed berm and a bully truck while flipping off the driver also demands fine motor skills.

My Moab friends mostly complain about flats from goat heads or cactus spines. Up here, glass from broken whiskey bottles poses a considerable risk. (Some stores have specials on six-packs of hard liquor, so business is brisk.) Even on Alaska's main highways, potholes from frost heaves open unexpectedly like big-game pitfall traps. Snowplows can suffocate or filet you, or mangle your ride. Snowmachines and moose cross at unpredictable intervals, and in the dark, the ungulates may mistake bikers for rivals or possible mates. On the upside, nobody, not even the most desperate dirt bag, will steal a bike model called *Mountain Tamer*.

Though admittedly there is less topographic relief around Fairbanks compared to, say, Moab's Poison Spider Mesa trail, similar weight loss and aerobic workouts can be expected. This is mostly due to snowdrifts on the road and excessive sweating in bulky clothing. For extremists, there is the Iditabike, a 200-mile winter race following a historical dog-mushing route. (Bring pepper spray, to fend off marauding wolves.) It's not quite as fancy as Moab's Primal Quest, during which bikers with their mounts rappel off Gemini Bridges' sandstone arches, but in a pinch, it will do.

Let's not forget moments of transcendence either, those fractals of beauty that wait by the roadside. Snow dervishes spinning on blacktop. Gamboling ravens. Mock suns, from ice crystals quivering in the air. White bunnies or ermines, stiff and flattened as boards.... On days when I'm too chicken to face traffic I shortcut through the woods behind campus, bisecting moose tracks, tree shadows, and spokes of sunlight. (But it's really a tradeoff, because I risk altercations with cross-country skiers over their groomed trails.)

When rubbernecking for migrating geese and cranes that chevron the sky or feed in the Creamer's Field wetlands, be sure to keep an eye on the road.

I am not that exceptional, overall. While not quite as busy as Moab, Fairbanks hums with cold-weather biking activity. There's the French expatriate, an accomplished classical violinist, who hauls bags of dog food on a trailer, for the huskies that share his backwoods home. There's Bob, who is wearing felt Viking helmets he sews and who wraps birch bark around his bike frame, which appears cobbled together from saplings. Another guy pulls an enclosed trailer with a clear plastic window even at forty below. (Is he carrying babies in there?) My neighbor, a Zamboni driver at the ice arena in town, commutes to work on a bike with rearview mirrors and milk crates, wearing white, inflatable "bunny boots" and headphones....

With our snotsicles and waxy cheeks, our breaths' plumes, and hulking silhouettes, we may look like members of Scott's last expedition. But an inner flame fuels us, some deep down awareness and pride: what is sport for some is transport for others. Regardless of trends, we are biking cool.

Recovery

THE SCENE ON THE HIGHWAY'S exit ramp caught me off guard. A stout woman, in her sixties perhaps, with glasses and frizzed brown hair, dressed in sneakers, jeans, and a sweatshirt, stood away from her parked truck, transfixed by something in the grass. Bicycling closer, I noticed she was Native American and the object of her attention was a bird plump as a chicken and glossy as obsidian. Fascinated by all wildlife and fond of aerobatic clowns in particular, I stopped on the gravel shoulder. The raven's left wing dragged; feather tips skimmed the grass. The chisel bill hung ajar, as if its owner were panting, displaying the mouth's soft lining. With each blink, white nictitating membranes closed on the bird's eyeballs like camera apertures freeze-framing the world.

"It's injured." The woman stated the obvious. "I'm trying to take it to a vet."

I asked if she needed a hand, and she went to the truck, returning with a sweatshirt. Noon sun ironed my back, undeterred by clouds with gray guts that sagged toward the horizon. As cars sped by, curiosity flickered across the drivers' faces. Oblivious to the streaking of traffic and pain, the bird focused on the more imminent threat we represented. Each time the woman approached, it hopped beyond reach, tucking the hurt wing close to its body, as a person would a dislocated arm. Circling around, I distracted it long enough for the woman to throw the shirt over it. She stooped, nimbly for somebody so compact, and scooped up the raven before it could wiggle free.

We walked to her truck, whose door I opened.

"Would you like to come to the vet?" she asked. "You could hold it while I drive."

I wedged my bike and backpack full of groceries into the truck and got in. En route to the opposite end of town, she rang a friend who had worked in bird rehabilitation. She already had called that friend for advice as soon as she spotted the bird.

"I got it and am driving to the vet now. A guy is helping me."

Through fabric my fingertips sensed the bird's heart. Unable to tell terror from resignation, I listened to its labored breathing, worried that it might suffocate or overheat. A scaly leather foot, tipped with lacquered claws, had escaped from the wrap, and pressed onto my belly. Occasionally, as frost heaves or cracks in the pavement shook the truck, wings brushed against my breastbone like spruce boughs or a book page turning. I had never been that close to a raven before.

My grandmotherly accomplice, Margaret, recalled how she had trapped a raven by accident when she still lived in her village up north. She had been setting snares to catch rabbits; to her surprise a raven stepped into one of her loops. She released it and, getting stabbed in the process, came to respect the bird's moxie and imposing bill.

Research for a school paper she had to write turned up little scientific information, but Margaret unearthed a wealth of raven lore, knowledge rooted deeply in time, accounts and beliefs that branched far beyond North America into Siberia and Europe.

Charcoal sketches in the caves near Lascaux depict corvids that imply messengers or human souls. Two ravens named Thought and Memory perched on Odin's shoulders, gleaning news of the world on daily excursions. And without stars to guide them through summer's nacreous midnights, Norse settlers released *hrafnar* and trailed the black scouts landward in their single-mast ships.

Throughout the northern hemisphere this bird attended shamanistic flights of trance. It was teacher and totemic ancestor. It stared bug-eyed from the limbs of family trees along the Pacific Northwest coast, populating genealogies hewn into cedar trunks. Kwakiutl dancers acknowledged the bond by wearing masks with four-foot-long bills that closed with whip crack sounds. Crow-walking under the spell of gourd rattles, they *became* birds. Other raven masks split like seedpods, revealing a second mask and thus the deception of first impressions, the hidden nature of things. In the mythology of Margaret's own people, the Gwich'in of the Yukon and northeast Alaska, Raven acted as trickster and transformer. In the course of his exploits, he often suffered violence or deformity, comparable to the bird I was cradling. Vulgar and petty, scheming and greedy and often not very smart, he embodied the sacred and the profane, the light and the shadow inside each one of us. At the beginning of "Distant Time," he created not only humans, but also animals, some of which looked after people as guardian spirits. As part of a bargain between species, people honored obligations, obeyed unwritten rules, and offered gestures of attentiveness, feeding dried fish to a wolf they had killed, or not disturbing a raven on its nest, lest the weather would turn cold. In an age that for believers is present to the same degree that it is past, Raven stole daylight for his creations, which until then scrambled around in the dark. Inspired perhaps by the bird's love for shiny objects or by a solar eclipse, one tale passed on over midwinter fires recounts Raven's theft of the sun. A chief in the sky had given the orb to his child as a toy. When the toddler dropped it and it rolled into the room's corner, Raven covered its glow with his wing. Then he flew back to earth with it, illuminating the world of people. His benevolence still can assume the form of ravens that guide hunters to fresh wolf kills, moose or caribou, the bounty of which feeds entire families. Villagers in Alaska pay close attention to the living environment, and a raven rolling onto its back in midair is "dropping a package of meat," announcing good fortune for the observant.

I told a few anecdotes of my own. On a snowy Fairbanks sidewalk I once found evidence of a raven meal: a scuffle of rune prints, banded feathers, and at the display's center a grouse foot. During a Grand Canyon trip, fat twin marauders in search of food hacked into my backpack and pulled out smelly socks. (I had been mad enough to fling rocks at them.) Similarly, a mile above timberline on Denali's buttressed heights, ravens had made the connection between bamboo wand markers and the food caches climbers left in a snowdrift, excavating peanuts, cheese, and beef jerky with great gusto. The climbers considered them flying rats, but people besides me have a soft spot for them. In downtown Sitka, I saw car drivers wait patiently for ravens to grab a meal on rain-slicked Harbor Drive instead of honking their horns or trying to squeeze by or to run over them.

Margaret and I realized we had common acquaintances in a city of 70,000 that can be as tight as a village, among them my former Native-language teacher. Our conversation, which had begun as a trickle, meandered around the invalid bird and its kin before, widening, the current roiled raw stuff to the surface.

Between raven stories nestled Margaret's confession that she was a recovering alcoholic. She hinted at divorce, at a step- or adoptive parent. Her children and grandchildren lived as far away as Tucson, and she rarely saw them. Beadworking had given her strength to pull through. "It keeps my hands and mind busy all the time," she told me. She talked about her style, how she kept seeing images and patterns in nature, which she then translated into art. Craft and expertise ran strong in Margaret's family. Her mother had passed on the gift; at age fourteen, she had fashioned a fringed, shell-and-bead-encrusted hide shirt for Margaret's great-grandfather, a chief. It now hung in a display case at the university museum on the hill above town—a flash from the well of history, a snippet of culture enshrined.

When we finally reached the clinic, the raven felt heavy and warm, like a swaddled, if flawed, foundling. The weight on my belly tapped a fount of nurturing that, for a non-pet person sworn to childlessness, welled up unexpectedly. I imagined how easily an observer could have mistaken our trio for a family rushing its infant to an emergency room.

There was an entrance for dogs and another for cats, but none for birds. We stood in the air-conditioned office's neon glare, with sterile surfaces and posters that advertised pet health care pressing in on us. I sweated where the cotton bundle touched my body. Margaret tugged on her T-shirt, admitting coolness to her skin. While a receptionist had her fill out some paperwork, my arms tired, and I braced them on the Formica counter. The bird squirmed again and let out a rusty squawk; I tried to keep a good grip, mindful not to break feathers or injure it even more.

Before long, a veterinarian's assistant took it into another room. She returned to hand Margaret her soiled sweatshirt.

"I'll have to wash this," Margaret said calmly.

"What will become of the bird?" I asked the receptionist before we left.

"The vet will see what she can do," she said. "We'll check with a rehabilitation place here in town, and when the bird is ready it will be released where you found it."

Back at the truck Margaret volunteered to drive me home. On the way there we talked some more. I wondered aloud if it was even legal to pick up or keep wildlife. "Let 'em come find me, if they want," was all she said. Before I stepped from the truck, Margaret showed me photos of her traditional yet innovative beadwork, paraphernalia of many-hued glass that she sold at church bazaars: garlands offsetting inspirational poems, necklaces culminating in bear pendants, tanned-hide discs blushing with floral designs, and wall hangings embroidered with the sign of her people's adopted faith. I asked for her phone number in case I ever needed a customized gift.

As much as I intended to let Margaret know the outcome of our rescue mission, I also needed to follow this story to its end for personal reasons. My writing, if not my curiosity, had almost ground to a halt. The world did not seem to provide any new plots. Words did not come easily anymore and when they did, mimicked flowers pressed in a book more than they did the green fertile mess that threatened to swallow my yard. But the minute I closed the cabin door, I grabbed pen and paper, and sentences began to form.

Next day I rang the clinic to inquire about the patient's condition. The diagnosis was bleak and the outlook even more so. As the result of heavy trauma, typically caused by collisions with cars or windowpanes, the raven had broken a wing bone and dislocated a shoulder and would never fly again. It shared the fate of many residents-turned-trespassers, an opportunistic lot that includes ants, magpies, rats, coyotes, deer, and here in Alaska, gray jays, bald eagles, and bears. Lacking foresight to dodge development as well as familiarity with technology's traps these camp followers glean from our tables, our henhouses, our backyards, our interstates. Who hasn't seen sly raven moves outside of supermarkets? Who hasn't seen them dive into greasy Dumpsters, haggle over scraps, or, heads cocked sideways, gauge the speed of traffic before dashing onto asphalt to peel off mangled rabbit flesh? We've created predator-free havens filled with tidbits and trash, and they flock to them. Such scavenging devalues them in the eyes of some people, who regard them as vermin. But is the ravens' defiance of human plans and conventions not wildness of a particular kind?

Some creatures have become so familiar that we no longer perceive them. They blend into the landscape as if plumage or fur were a camouflage coat. When we *do* take notice, we sometimes label them "common," but there is nothing common about this rogue bird, except for its manners. Of all our wild neighbors it is the one that most reminds us of ourselves.

At Prudhoe Bay's oil fields, ravens begin to nest in late March, at minus thirty degrees. With no twigs free of snow, they requisition unusual nest-building material: welding rods, plastic cable ties, copper wires, survey stakes. Some assemble to meet incoming cargo, waiting at the airstrip for the plane's arrival. During the unloading, they raid food crates, rip open the packaging, and sometimes hide loot in industrial structures, away from patrolling foxes. As soon as the snow melts, they waddle after lemmings; they pilfer eggs and chicks from migratory birds. They mostly ignore oil field workers but avoid the researcher who previously trapped them, with paper lunch bags as bait, recognizing the enemy even when she wears borrowed coveralls and a hard hat in disguise.

Ravens handle cold snaps of minus fifty degrees or below far better than they do cars. Their physiology enables them to prosper anywhere between the Sonoran Desert and the Arctic Ocean. Reminiscent of Raven's mythic coup, they capture minute amounts of sunlight with their dark, absorbent plumage and, fluffed up, retain precious body heat. Sheer size, combined with stockiness, helps these largest of passerines to preserve life under winter's coarse cloak. On clear winter days you can surprise ravens with fanned wings sunbathing on the ground or rolling exuberantly in heavenly down. If you sit still enough, long enough, in a Fairbanks parking lot, vignettes of urban raven life will accumulate: Seven birds aligned on the back of a truck, eyeing its garbage-strewn bed and clucking at the sudden bonanza. A pair locked together in midair, tumbling tails-over-heads, scattering feathers as if in a pillow fight. A scruffy loner extracting ketchup packets from a plastic bag, stashing them in snow piled around the foot of a parking meter for future consumption. They live like street bums or heroes fallen from grace; some people take this as a sign that the ancient spirits no longer care for their animal manifestations. Fledged under Alaska's raw skies, the birds still belong more in this place than I, a transplant from afar.

In Distant Time stories, the trickster and culture hero often tripped over his own appetites. Left alone, its descendant, the specimen we had brought in, also was likely to meet a bad end. It would starve or fall to the next predator crossing its path. The vet was still trying to contact the only qualified bird rehabilitator in town. If that person could not give it refuge, the raven would be euthanized. Appalled by the news, I wanted to take it home but discovered I needed a permit and appropriate setup for keeping a wild animal. The vet refused to turn loose the bird and, detecting my frustration with clinic protocol, reminded me that I had interfered with nature's workings when I helped retrieve it. But I'd stepped in only because our kind caused the accident in the first place.

I called again the following day, a Sunday. The receptionist kept me in a limbo of Muzak laced with commercials. When she came back on the line, she informed me that the bird had been put down. I pictured the vet thrusting a syringe through the iridescent mantle into warm flesh I had held. As jet-button eyes lost their luster, I wished for one less story to tell.

When I phoned Margaret at work the next morning, she had already heard about the mercy killing. "Too bad," she said while I held on to the receiver. Regret and compassion colored her voice, and an entire life's weight rested upon those two words.

Honeymoon for Three

BELOW US, A TUNDRA MOSAIC unfolds in 100 hues of brown and green, splotched with the unblinking blue of melt-water ponds. Frost heaves or *pingos* blister the land, interrupting its polygonal patterns. Willow patches cling to rivers whose braids unravel with distance. Above the horizon, the peaks of northern Alaska's Brooks Range hover like long-held wishes come true.

Our pilot Bob is an old hand—a "sourdough" as they call them up here—with the frame and facial hair of a griz. He turns to me, nods. I can see myself duplicated in his insect-eye aviator glasses, dwarfed by the immensity outside the cockpit. A toothy grin splits his furry face.

My brother, his new wife, and I took the regular twin-prop from Fairbanks, where I was waiting for my summer guiding schedule to fill. On its way north, the plane crossed the Yukon River thousands of feet above the pipeline filled with buried sunlight from Prudhoe Bay. Whittling away at pale, spruce-covered bluffs, the great river rolled placidly westward to its appointment with the Bering Sea. After a brief stop in Bettles, on the airfield that served as a way station for U.S. warplanes sent to Russia during World War II, we switched to Bob's single-engine Cessna with floats, chartered through an outfitter.

"So, when are you guys gonna be at the Alatna?" our pilot comes in over my headset, between bouts of static.

I shudder and roll my eyes to get my brother's attention.

"What do you mean, 'Alatna?' We were planning to hike to the John, where you are supposed to drop off our boats and supplies for the river leg of this trip."

"Right. No problem," drawls the voice in my ear.

He pulls on the horn, the plane banks into a steep easterly turn, and gravity pushes me into the seat. On the instrument panel, the artificial horizon is tilting like unbalanced scales when the stalling alarm goes off. I catch a glimpse of my brother. His eyes seem to plead. I hope you know what you are doing, they say.

They are on their honeymoon, Andrew and Kerstin, my pert, curly-haired sister-in-law. This is to be the adventure heralding an even bigger one: a life spent together. I know the area between Gates of the Arctic National Park and the middle reaches of the Koyukuk River from my research in several Native communities and agreed to be their guide—on the ground and water, but not up here. They are kin, and I hold myself responsible for their safety and wellbeing. Right now, I worry about the male gene pool of our family evaporating in a big ball of fire.

Before long, the plane loses altitude, diving straight for a chain of glacial lakes that separates foothills and plains from the gray granite of the Endicott Mountains. I crane my neck to scan the slopes on my side for wildlife. Bob zeroes in on one of the glassy surfaces. When the floats touch down, spray obliterates our bird's shadow on the water. With the engine throttled, we taxi to shore.

As we unload backpacks and sort through piles of food, I notice movement from the corner of my eye. Turning toward it, I catch a stately caribou bull splashing into the shallows before throwing itself into the deep. It cuts straight across the lake, and the V of its wake twinkles in the rich afternoon light. Only the head and sweep of antlers are showing, like forked driftwood. Not far behind, a grizzly comes crashing through the underbrush, desperate for a meal. The ease and speed of this bolt of taut muscle are breathtaking—at a short distance, it could out-gallop a horse. Without hesitation, Old Ephraim plunges in and streaks after the bull.

"I'll keep her running," Bob shouts over the engine's growling, "Just in case." Dumbstruck and momentarily frozen in place, all three of us think that this is a good idea.

By the time Andrew has rummaged through his backpack and pulled out the camera, the bear and its intended dinner are too far away for a decent shot. When I clip the economy-size can of pepper spray to my pack, it seems awfully puny.

"Got your hot sauce," Bob jokes, "to spice up his dinner?" I think he means us.

Before we part, I point out the rendezvous place to him on the map.

"See you guys in a week, then."

"Headwaters of the John!"

"The John. Right."

We shake his callused paw, and watch as he folds his bulk back into the cockpit.

Too soon for us to feel ready, the engine's droning ebbs and dies, and the plane shrinks to a speck in the distance. Only the smell of kerosene lingers. Silence reigns again, accentuated by the whine of mosquitoes. Worn out from two flights and spooked by our introduction to nature's way of doing business, we decide to spend the night here. While Kerstin and I set up the tents, "Robert Redford" assembles his rod and reel and starts casting for grayling or trout.

"You might want to put on some bug dope, or better yet, gloves and a hat," I say.

"In a minute. Just a few more."

We end up having good old mac-n'-cheese, without fish, inside their roomy honeymoon suite. My brother's hands are almost too swollen to hold a spoon. His usually gaunt face looks puffy and flushed, and I bet he is running a temperature.

"Told you so, city slicker."

"Whatever."

Later, stretched out in my pup tent, I contemplate our arrival. Hard to believe that only this morning, I awoke in a bed in the city. Through my fly screen I watch a lazy sun grazing the world's edge without ever dipping below. Light dense and golden as mead floods the enclosed space. Shadows on the ground outside mimic the lengthening summer days. The sky glows lavender, unencumbered by clouds, while famished hordes hit the tent fly, sounding like rain.

Our route to the headwaters is a treeless *Via Dolorosa*. Distance north of the Arctic Circle often is measured in pints of sweat and blood. We mostly hike looking like beekeepers, dolled-up in rain gear, gaiters, gloves, head nets, and hats, with temperatures approaching ninety degrees Fahrenheit. The only alternative is an insect repellent with DEET, a chemical compound the Army developed after the Pacific War. Its side effects can include hallucinations, insomnia, mood disturbances, and seizures, a few of which have ended in death. It dissolves plastic zippers and leather and is probably a derivative of DDT or Agent Orange. People with PhDs worked on this "Jungle Juice"—the bugs seem to like it. There is no kissing with this bitter stuff on; fearing weird side effects and planning to have healthy offspring, the newlyweds stay chaste, at least to my knowledge. Indian old-timers have told me that, to keep mosquitoes away, they would carry a can of smoldering tree fungus in the bottom of their boats. But there's no tree fungus to be found here, because there are no trees.

Boots are forever soaked in this marshy terrain—squish,

squish, squish…squelch goes the soundtrack for our hike. Only surface layers of soil thaw under the 24/7 stare of the Arctic midsummer sun. Because the permafrost underneath never melts, water pools on the tundra with nowhere to drain—perfect breeding grounds for the beasts. Atop this gigantic sponge, we barely find enough level, dry ground to pitch our tents. When there are no mosquitoes, horseflies the size of June bugs plague us, or else tiny no-see-'ums. The insects appear to be working in shifts. On a good day, there are flies. Each night, before we slip into our sleeping bags, we check for mold growing between our toes.

Tussocks promise dry crossings of the soggy flats, but walking on them resembles balancing on camel humps. Stepping into the mud pockets in-between is not a good option either; it feels like post-holing in snow, and boots get soaked within minutes. Stepping dead center onto the mop heads seems the trick to avoid sprained ankles and wet feet. But with each step a voracious cloud lifts from a tussock. Every few hundred yards I need to stop, wheezing like an asthmatic. I am also miffed that I have to take in the scenery filtered through a head net. (After Andrew developed the photos from our trip, he found most of them ruined, stippled with dots like black snow.)

We've perfected the "cook dinner dressed to the gills and dive headlong into the tent without spilling the beans" act, and by now, it has become routine. Before we even sample the first spoonful of stews I concoct from dehydrated ingredients, we purge the tent of intruders. Bugs already sated by *their* meal leave crimson smears on the tent walls when we squeeze life out of them. We learn that the big, clumsy ones that survived the winter are not nearly as agile or vicious or numerous as this year's batch. In the mornings, we break camp in a hurry to get moving and escape our pursuers for a while, literally itching to go.

Occasionally, I try to dish out more protracted punishment, using an apocryphal method of executing mosquitoes. You can supposedly tighten a muscle to prevent a sucking freeloader from withdrawing its stiletto proboscis from your skin. Your pumping heart will swell the bug's abdomen until it bursts like a tiny balloon, a death fit for gluttons. After repeated attempts, I find that I am more likely to bust a blood vessel or suffer a hernia from the strain. There is no consolation either in knowing that I just volunteered nourishment for another generation of tormentors.

Make no mistake; these are not your garden-variety mosquitoes—they rank among the fiercest and most prolific of North America's 150 species. A fellow diarist described their predecessors in the Klondike goldfields, more than a hundred years ago:

> They are not like the usual mosquito. They light and bite in the same instant, never lose any time in feeling around.... In panning, we sometimes have them light on the back of the bare hand so thick that instantly the hand is black with them and we scrape them off the same way we would mud or other soft stuff. Plunging the hand in water will not dislodge those that have a good hold.

Gone are the times when we joked about Alaska's vampire "state birds," or the leg-hold-trap key rings to capture them that Fairbanks curio shops sell. The single-strike kill record on our trip stands at thirty-four. My Buddhist leanings notwithstanding, I have become used to the sound of one hand slapping. This is nothing but good old, eye-for-an-eye revenge, a vendetta with the divine: "He sent among them swarms of flies, which devoured them"—*Psalms* 78:45.

In a place where storytelling explains the world and alleviates endless, dark nights, people remember how mosquitoes first came to be. According to one myth, an Eskimo man stabbed a cannibal monster after learning about its Achilles' heel. "Though

I am dead," the giant said, "I will keep on eating you and all other humans forever." To prevent this, the man cut the body into pieces, which he burned in a fire. When he tossed the resulting ashes into the wind, each flake became a mosquito.

Modern science does not tell fables about the bugs' origins, but it can give us a handle on quantities. An entomologist calculated for me the mass of mosquitos in Alaska, with equations that made my brain hurt. The annual crop of the devil's seed, according to him, weighs roughly ninety-six million pounds, the equivalent of human biomass in the state.

Over dinner one evening, I wonder aloud what the masses eat when we're not around. "Caribou," my brother says. And he's right. Feasting mosquitoes draw up to a quart of blood per week from a hapless animal, and backpackers find rotting carcasses that have been completely drained. A bush pilot I know gives graphic accounts of mosquito rapaciousness: surveying large caribou herds from the air, he's seen engorged swarms spatter his plane's windows like blood rain. Increasing in numbers as the climate warms, mosquitoes even drive breeding birds from their nests and attack their naked feet, which, according to one researcher, can make them look like "fur slippers." But at least we are spared botflies and warble flies, whose larvae digest the tissue of nasal passages and emerge from the backs of living caribou.

Scratching my bites till they're raw, it helps to see the good in even these pests. Without them, and without winter's dark moods, Alaska would be as crowded as Colorado or Wyoming, playgrounds for the newly rich and eternally bored. Like bears, those largest predators on the tundra, the smallest ones keep us humble. They remind us that we are still part of the food chain, and not necessarily at the top. In a beautiful democracy of predation, mosquitoes feed on grizzlies as well as on us; their pond-born larvae, myriads of wriggling question marks, in turn sustain thousands of shorebirds and their chicks.

The nearly featureless landscape that harbors mosquito eggs

throughout subzero winters keeps unfurling, doing its best to deny us progress. With nothing but nondescript hills around, it is hard to identify landmarks for taking compass bearings, and the maps often are no help. We zig and then zag repeatedly, attempting to correct our course. At some point, Kerstin throws down her pack, sits on a hummock, and breaks into tears.

"Wilderness—I had no idea what you meant." "No trails—anywhere. I want trees!"

I feel sorry for her. At times like these, I feel sorry for myself.

For good measure, the only non-stinging wildlife we encounter after our run-in at the lake is a solitary moose. It looks scrawny enough to act as a double for the one from the opening credits of *Northern Exposure.*

More than a week and who knows how many miles later, we top yet another rise of the oceanic expanse. Below us, Paradise: stunted Christmas trees, the first black spruce since we left Fairbanks. A lake tucked into a silvery crook of the John River. Finally! The put-in for the river leg of our journey. We may be running a day or two late; we don't know exactly. The only watch we carry does not show dates. Time's fun when you're having flies. Close to shore, we come upon two canoes with the outfitter's logo, several bear-proof barrels of food, and, I hope, a shipment from the blood bank.

Bless your heart, Bob.

After a layover day at the depot, splurging on fresh veggies and fruit, resting sore muscles, and airing out feet, we take some practice turns on the lake. Neither one of the honeymooners has ever been in a canoe. Afterward, we portage to the river, load up, and shove off. By the time we join the main current, the bugs have let up considerably.

The honeymoon, however, is far from over.

Andrew and Kerstin share one canoe, while I paddle the other. Or try to. A few strokes out, I realize that the load is unbalanced, too far back in the boat and listing to starboard. The bow is too light, which becomes a problem when a headwind starts up. Gusts spin the canoe like a compass needle until it points upriver—due north. I curse and swear and keep turning it downstream, falling quickly behind. Upset, I paddle frantically, uncoordinated, only to capsize. My breath catches high in my chest and a second distends to contain—everything. I take a mouthful of John River that is half ice water, half glacial silt.

As soon as we've righted the boat and fished my sodden belongings from an eddy, we re-shuffle the seating arrangements. All three of us now ride in one canoe, with myself in the middle. Around these parts, this is known as the "missionary position." In the old days, greenhorns in black robes and clutching bibles always rode mid-ship, while their stoic-faced Native guides propelled the craft with deft strokes, biting their lips to keep from laughing. We hitch the second canoe to our stern with its bowline, towing it along. Here we are, three white folks coming down the river, one sopping wet, all looking like fools. But at the moment, nobody seems to be watching.

I am having a bad flashback to a solo trip on the Noatak River the year before. Rounding a bend, I'd come face to face with a grizzly and her cub. They were swimming across the narrow channel, ears and black noses poking from the water. The current kept sweeping me onward, swiftly and relentlessly, despite much frantic backpaddling. I was clearly set on a collision course. The mother took one good look, judged both trajectories, and decided to return to the side from which they had come. Back on the cutbank she shook her massive head, shedding water in a halo of droplets like an overgrown Saint Bernhard. One last glance over her shoulder, and she'd sauntered off into the bushes, her fuzzy offspring glued to her heels.

The scenario of a snarling mess of bear, rope, honeymooners, and boats so far from help brings cold sweat to my brow.

Several miles downstream, we are well into the tree line.

Because we are no longer used to vegetation higher than knee level, the sky appears pinched and somehow diminished. The stream roils complacently under our keels, slipping across gravel bars, wheeling around bends, weaving and murmuring, grabbing clods of dirt here and there, unhurried, but preoccupied with its destination. It leaves sandbars exposed, vibrating fallen trees as it passes. Such "strainers" can easily become deathtraps, pinning or flipping canoes and pushing swimmers' heads underwater. The *whack!* of a beaver's tail feels like a slap in the face, asking me to pay attention. The sound almost makes me drop my paddle, but the culprit remains invisible.

Days later, we pull out at the confluence of the John and the Koyukuk River. Bettles, a village of forty, lies several miles upstream from this junction. We could line our canoes along the Koyukuk's brushy banks, but I decide to forego the ordeal and blow a wad of cash instead.

"Let's call a taxi," I say.

"Have you been drinking?" Andrew asks, concern rumpling his face. He knows I don't have a satellite phone or even a cell phone or landline.

Near a meat cache on stilts and a log cabin, I locate the weatherproof box I knew would be there, clamped to the trunk of a tall spruce. An antenna extends above the tree's top, and a solar panel close by fuels the contraption. Hi-tech has found its way into the bush. I open the box, lift the receiver, and almost instantly talk to our outfitter in Bettles.

"I'll be there in an hour," he says and hangs up.

"Another chatterbox," I mutter to myself.

"I wonder if you could have ordered us pizza," Kerstin chimes in.

Soon after we have finished unloading the canoes, a decked aluminum skiff rounds a bend in the river. With it, noise has returned. But we relish the moment, ready for beer, a shower, and a bunk bed, in that order.

"Guess you found the boats alright," our chauffeur greets us, throwing me a line.

We strap both canoes to the skiff's cabin roof and take off. As the boreal forest zips by in a blur and the wind musses my hair, an emotion like regret washes over me. It could be a long time before I find myself up north again, if ever, as life has a tendency to intervene with even our best-laid plans. Despite the past weeks' discomforts, I feel that something profound has ended. But for the lovebirds reclining on the front deck, wrapped up in fleece jackets and conversation, this is just the beginning.

Notes from the Road to Bestsellerdom

I HAD PLANNED THE PROMO TOUR for a collection of northern wildlife stories I'd edited like a field marshal plans a campaign. A four-day Book Blitz South would target eight locations in the Anchorage and Mat-Su area: independent and chain bookstores, a café, a museum, a luncheon for professional communicators, and a nature center up in the mountains. In preparation, flyers had been printed and hung, emails and press kits sent, and the events listed in several papers as well as online. Reservations had been made at a cozy but pricey downtown B&B, at my, not the publisher's expense. The publicist had worked overtime, constructing a collapsible poster stand from struts, spars, screws, and an old lamp foot; the book's cover printed on cloth, in San Francisco, no less, could be hoisted on this contraption like a sail on a mast.

I realize that words alone rarely draw crowds any more, unless you're a politician. Authors on book tours are therefore encouraged to play Indian flutes, tap-dance, wear clown suits, juggle their books blindfolded, or at least to behave inappropriately. I enlisted support troops, inviting writers who had contributed pieces to the anthology. Owls and falcons were to deliver the coup de grace. The presence of live raptors and their handlers from two rehabilitation facilities was no mere publicity stunt. My failed raven rescue in Fairbanks had inspired the story collection, and one contributor's essay described the visit of an education bird (Gandalf, a great gray owl crippled in an accident) to her eco-literature class. I admired these volunteers and their wards, and piggybacking their act with mine was supposed to benefit everybody involved. My girlfriend, who also happened to be the book's designer, acted as liaison, trip photographer, finance officer, driver (I haven't driven since 1980), quartermaster, and motivational coach wrapped into one.

As we rolled into town, thousands of animal lovers thronged the streets. Alas, they had come to see—dogs.

In my ignorance of Alaska pastimes, I had overlooked that the Book Blitz weekend coincided with the Iditarod, the world's most prestigious sled dog race. At the B&B, all the other guests turned out to be volunteer dog handlers, one a British police officer visiting from Hong Kong. Another Husky groupie, a Connecticut retiree, had attended the race start eight years in a row. None quite struck me as "the literary type." Still, the outdoor theme and commercial vibe were encouraging, and we promptly spotted some wildlife fans in the crowd: predator-hating Sarah Palin and a bearded guy wearing a wolf-pelt hood complete with the animal's head, glassy-eyed and fangs bared.

I was hoping a trickle-down from the human surge would reach bookstores between the ceremonial ("fake" according to hardcore mushing aficionados) race start and the time when the bars would get busy.

The luncheon at a posh hotel seemed an auspicious beginning. My choice of reading, the story of Bart and his foraging escapades, elicited gasps, eye-rolling and even chuckles, but might have curbed book sales somewhat. The audience of silver-maned professionals looked as if they knew their *coq au vin* from their *bouillabaisse*.

The campus bookstore looked deserted, as most students had already left for spring break. The museum was being renovated, and foot traffic through the echoing lobby, behind the owl's back, made the bird nervous and incontinent. A guy on crutches parked himself in front of my table. "Glad they didn't put you upstairs." He commenced telling me his lengthy medical history, then limped away without buying a book. Each signing appears to attract one of these attention hogs, and I'm convinced they are taking turns.

The chain-store manager put me in a prime spot, at a table facing the entrance, where I could make eye contact with customers as they entered. Light from the low-angle sun made me squint like a shortsighted bookworm (not look sharp-eyed as a wilderness guide and auteur should) or, when I tried to remedy that, glower like a sun-glassed Mafioso. With each gust from the sliding doors, my poster swiveled on its stand, causing the printed grizzly to scan the room as if in search of prey. The store policy did not allow raptors to be brought in, for liability reasons. I felt rather lonely without a feathered companion.

The large, independent, downtown store had advertised a panel discussion of the book. Unfortunately only one of my authors showed up—and didn't reveal her presence until after my improvised reading. Her friends made up the bulk of the audience, literally, as fishermen and fisherwomen are put together impressively. The performance took place in the kids' books section, where I wrestled with a defective microphone. Trying to maintain eye contact while keeping close to the too-low mike, I felt like Quasimodo talking out of the side of his mouth. Book clerks shook their heads as squeals of electronic feedback filled the place. The birds, as always, drew scores of youngsters and their cash-carrying guardians.

At the café, wired on complimentary caffeine and with my voice beginning to sound like a raven's, I worked hard to be heard over the coffee grinder and hissing espresso machine.

The next day, the action and masses moved on to the real race start at Willow, and we joined the traffic creeping north. The Eagle River Nature Center was a retreat from urban mayhem, a Zen oasis for birdwatchers. The turnout was good. When I opened the floor for questions, a kid in the first row who had endured my reading, piped up, "When do we get to touch the owl?" "We don't," the bird handler snapped. The owl was not in a petting mood. Halfway through the presentation, it had noticed a stuffed eagle with fully spread wings, mounted below the log ceiling; it went into a hooting frenzy and kept diving off the handler's leather glove, flapping upside down because it was leashed. It had to be put back in its cage. No doubt, these animals remained wild; they lit up the indoors with their own kind of electricity, a white-hot intensity that still sparks in us.

At our final venue, a bookstore-cum-café north of Anchorage, the manager had expected a signing, not a reading. There were no chairs for an audience, and I found myself separated from the handlers and their birds by a shelf full of gewgaws. (Has anyone else noticed how these increasingly augment book sales?) In a last-ditch, desperate bid for customer attention, I rearranged some books on a shelf, placing my brainchild between two local bestsellers—one, a biography of our "Mama grizzly" then-governor—hoping to profit by proximity.

After two hours of signing, or rather non-signing, I had sold five books total, four of those to the bird handlers. Because each bed within a 200 mile radius had been claimed for the night and we had no reservations, my girlfriend and I hit the road around sundown, trying to make Fairbanks that night. Near Denali State Park, snowflakes caught in our headlights and rushing toward the windscreen began to resemble galaxies seen at warp speed. Black ice on the road glared like a disgruntled publisher. We pulled out near some trailhead and fretted for a few hours, cramped in the back of the Subaru, between boxes of unsold books, waiting for dawn to come.

Descending the last hill into Fairbanks bleary-eyed-from our drive, I let the trip pass in review. Perhaps I did compete with myself, pitting wild animals against words about wild animals, a contest I can't ever and possibly shouldn't win. The timing could have been better, the audience more receptive, the arrangements with store managers and owners bomb-proofed beforehand.

But in a strange M. C. Escher effect, like two hands drawing each other, the book had spawned more animal and people moments, encounters around which one could build whole new stories, and that had made the trip worth our while:

The gap-toothed teenager from Anaktuvuk, telling of the wolf that bit his grandfather.

The grandmother, mother, and daughter trio—diligent bird-watchers all.

The bird handler-airplane mechanic who cleans cages and shows birds after work and talked about going back to school to become a raptor biologist.

The reader who complimented us on the book's cover and typography.

The naturalist-volunteer at the nature center, unwrapping his copy of *Walden*, prefaced and signed by Edward Abbey as if it were an icon.

And, just as impressive:

The merlin that had helped its presenter to overcome her fear of public speaking.

The great horned owl, mesmerizing kids with its yellow gaze.

The northern saw-whet owl, blind in one eye, elflike on its handler's fist.

The red-tail that, after suffering gunshot wounds, learned to trust humans.

Regardless of how many or few books were sold that time

around, I could hope that our stories, like these birds, would touch someone's life, somewhere.

I later heard from a friend who used my essay from the book to teach nature writing to students in China, and I wondered what they made of grizzly-polar bear hybrids in the Arctic. How did the unknown creatures quicken in their imagination? Strangely, my words traveled farther than I ever did, spiraling outward, released from my care like bold, salvaged birds.

Berry-Pickers and Earthmovers

I KNEEL ON THE SLOPE BELOW Newton Peak, outside of Nome, where my girlfriend got a job as a public health nurse. One hand cupped in berry bushes, I receive the land's ample gifts.

Sunshine massages my shoulders while incense of crushed Labrador tea rises from the warm tundra. Claret-colored blueberry leaves, orange dwarf birch, and bearberry, crimson as freshly spilled blood, mingle in fall's high-latitude quilt. I delicately strip berries from twigs, letting them roll into my palm before placing handfuls into a yogurt container. This late in the season, the plump flesh bursts easily, staining my fingertips purple. The fruits' signature hue, a pale, dusty indigo rarely encountered in nature, surprises and then reels you in; their scattershot growth pulls you farther and farther as hours slip away unnoticed.

Lulled by the meditative activity, I pop a few berries into my mouth, where tartness explodes like insight between my palate and tongue. Most blueberries sold in stores pale by comparison; obese and engineered into blandness, they betray an obsession with quantity, a disregard for season and place. One Fairbanks friend crushes such cultivars to dye skeins of wool, which hard-core gourmets consider the only use.

Not a good berry-year, this one—few sunny days in the past months. My bucket fills very slowly. People have flown up from Anchorage, because throughout south-central Alaska cater-pillars have been shredding berry bushes. More than usual, information about productive patches has been guarded like insider-trading tips, shared only with friends. Blueberries are selling for twenty dollars a quart through our town's online exchange network, often to locals too busy or impatient to pick. Regardless of the shortage, I shun berry combs, the plastic-and-steel gadgets that mimic bear claws, because they bruise fruit, damage bushes, and collect too much debris. They keep me from handling the velvety spheres, and their efficiency strikes me as semi-industrial. Berry picking appeals to me for its humbling pace, its quiet thrift. It requires no fancy tools—no fishing rods, four-wheelers, high-powered rifles, or outboard motors—and no logistics or permits, just an old bucket and a strong back.

Far out, afloat on sheet-metal glare, barge-like gold dredges sift Nome's ancient beaches, submerged when ice sheets melted and the sea repossessed land at the end of the Pleistocene. Belch-es and growls from heavy machinery waft up with an onshore breeze. A belt of scars girdles foothills below, outlining an even older beach and placer-rich stream gravel buried beneath glacial till. Earthmovers and caterpillars are scraping the gold-bearing layers, throwing up molehills of human industry. Dwarfing all present-day efforts, long-necked, turn-of-the-century dredges wallow in marsh ponds like doomed brontosauruses.

A quirky town with a makeshift feel, Nome still attracts dreamers and schemers. It's a lot like Cicely, the setting of *North-ern Exposure*, only less photogenic, much rougher around the edges. Curbside dredge buckets planted with flowers pass for beautification here, and the world's largest gold pan, vis-à-vis the Methodist church, resembles a UFO driven partway into the balding lawn. At low tide, swigging oblivion from brown paper bags, the uprooted stand around driftwood fires behind the revetment where, despite the dike's granite boulders, the sea tries to steal from the shore. Up-valley from wind turbines that flash with each revolution, some bright satanic mill disembowels Mount Brynteson. With the economy's nosedive, gold has reached an all-time high, renewing the frenzy for pay dirt: a blueberry-sized nugget is worth 1,200 dollars.

Fortunes made, fortunes missed, lives spent pawing the ground, and a few miners breaking even. Stuffy and dark as animal dens, the bars along Front Street stay busy, as does the town's only bank, handing out berry buckets with its logo as if promoting frugality. The payback as well as the scale of extraction differs, but diggers and pickers like myself equally feed desire, not need. Secretive and territorial, we move on when the yields no longer warrant the effort. Quitting is hard. As the year tilts into winter, the berries turn mushy; earth and sea harden to human intrusion, frost and ice put our ambition on hold.

Typically seen as women's business, berry picking lacks the excitement of striking gold or of killing a moose, except when blundering into a grizzly with a sweet tooth in your chosen patch. Berry size simply does not matter as much as nugget or rack size. As a rule, swamps, rivers, and mountain ranges need not be crossed chasing fruit. No guts, no glory. Not bringing home bacon. Men stalk—women stoop. Alas, research has shown that in some hunter-gatherer societies plants contribute most of the calories and prove more reliable than migratory game.

Comparing mental maps of both foraging sexes also made clear that they lived in different worlds: weighed down by toddlers, women knew smaller, nearer places more intimately, while men, unencumbered and perhaps rushed to return, excelled at memorizing long-distance trails and trade routes but in less detail.

It is tempting, from this perspective, to contemplate domestic dynamics, attitudes toward the settled and the unsettled (or the unsettling), the bird in the hand and the birds in the bush. My girlfriend, for instance, loves combing the outskirts of town, looking for muskox wool, mushrooms, or chips of opaque beach glass, turquoise and cobalt, the kinds no longer made. Although she's an avid hiker, an evening stroll through the neighborhood suits her just fine. She can pore for hours over seed catalogues. Not the homebuilder or handyman type, I've bunked in barracks, tents, monasteries, a guest ranch, log cabin, sauna, storage unit, stick lean-to, garage, various trailers, rock alcoves, the belly of a ferry, a houseboat on dry land, a survivalist's underground bunker, and a blue-tarp Tootsie Roll on the banks of the Rio Grande, all furnished minimally or not at all. Only half-joking, she accuses me of ADD and of having become jaded about small things in nature, such as birdsongs, snowflakes, or scents. It is true, I did inherit the restless gene, possibly from a great-grand uncle who sold the farm and joined a traveling circus. I crave a fresh view, forever following rivers, and piecing together new backpacking itineraries, big picture stuff. Even the flat prospect of a topo map tickles me. Luckily, the rewards of wild fruit, culinary and otherwise, prompt me to cherish the tangible and nearby, not just the abstract, faraway.

Back home, I carefully rinse leaf litter from my loot before freezing the berries in Ziplocs. (Better yet, let them gently roll down a towel slide to catch crud, the same principle as the miner's sluice box.) The local Inupiat stored their berries in skins bloated with seal oil, preventing spoilage and scurvy. Our stash likewise provides precious vitamins where produce is airlifted in and therefore expensive. In the bleak pit of December, when snow buries porches and winds moan like errant souls, our berry-inked lips mock hypothermia.

Cocooned in our kitchen, we relish summer's dense flavors, memories of lush life, nuggets of sunshine. We fold them into muffin and pancake batter, fill jam jars and piecrusts, or spoon them directly from a bag as a substitute for sorbet and lost daylight.

Berry picking can be many things to many people: livelihood, pastime, fresh-air therapy, pause for reflection or displacement activity, and even act of resistance. I distinctly remember a field trip with an ethnographer, a dead-ringer for Yul Brynner, to an Inupiaq village up the coast. He was grilling some grandmother in her single-room home who had dressed in her best *kuspuk*, about his pet theory: the existence of Eskimo clans before first contact with Anglo-Americans. Repeatedly, and with great patience, she denied ever having heard of such kin groups. When the researcher kept pressing, her gaze strayed out the window. "It's such a nice day," she said sweetly. "I think I'm going to look for berries."

On the year's last fishing trip to Council, I meet Cassie Walker, an Inupiaq elder with silver pageboy hair and piebald skin from vitiligo, like the worn-out salmon in the river's pools. She was born there, in a cabin above the Niukluk, during the Great Depression. As her mind peoples the near-ghost town with spirits, she points out who used to live where. Many of her parents' generation perished from ills dogging vagrant fortune seekers everywhere: the newcomers drove away game and introduced God, booze, and diseases. But berries kept bluing, in good as in bad years. In 1959, after boarding school in Sitka, Cassie moved to San Francisco, where she still lives. Now, perhaps for the last time, the old woman has come to this river, to claim days long gone, and the berries that mark vital ground.

Marginalia

> I devoted myself to simplicity and returned to it all, left that
> workaday life for this wisdom of wandering, for this wilderness
> of rivers-and-mountains clarity.

> —XIE LINGYUN (385–433 CE), *Dwelling in the Mountains*

I PUT THE MAPS OF MY ARCTIC traverse end to end, as I sometimes do, to relive the experience—all the wilderness I could
ever want spreads across my living room floor. Cleaved by glacial
valleys, shoaled by the Coastal Plain to the north and by boreal forest to the south, Alaska's stark Brooks Range spans the
state's entire width, a thousand miles east to west scaled down
here to just thirteen feet. To save weight on my sixty-day trek,
I had not brought notebooks but instead kept a journal on the
maps' backs and in their margins. The dot-and-dash line of the
Continental Divide, which I'd crossed numerous times, snakes
along the mountainous spine, sorting waters headed north, to
the Arctic Ocean, from those southbound for the Bering Strait.

The map sheets are battered, taped at the folds, as I consulted them often, and often in a drizzle, seeking guidance from these silent oracles. The occasional bloodstain or smushed mosquito speaks of torments at ground level. All formerly blank spaces now crawl with my handwriting, possibilities turned, if not into certainties, then at least into life in the guise of text—the work of a nature accountant or an ambulant graphomaniac. The map panels, too, are heavily annotated, with my symbols for food-and-fuel drops, gravel airstrips—a lifeline to civilization—and my route worming into the wilderness. The small tent-shape triangles of my campsites align like prayer beads shielding me from a harsh world; each one restores a sweet home away from home. Places I'd dreamed about before, with the help of my maps, cohered first as reality and too soon only as memories. What, from a pilot's perspective, resembled a hostile rucked labyrinth over time felt familiar as broken-in boots.

Uncluttered space, which I first perceived through maps and explorers' accounts, was part of the attraction that had brought me north. Every named mountain seemed to huddle among ten anonymous peaks that had possibly never been climbed. Spoken like mantras, the names themselves rang with visionary topographies, from Plunge Creek to Mount Deliverance, Frigid Crags, Old Woman Creek, and beyond. Each was whittled-down haiku poetry, a narrative in a nutshell. But I did not mistake the finger pointing at the moon for the moon, did not think this land could be learned through colorful maps alone.

I had first set foot in this territory more than two decades ago, as an anthropology student doing research. The National Park Service wanted to know which areas of Kobuk Valley and Gates of the Arctic national parks Inupiaq and Koyukon hunters and gatherers had used in the past. If those tribes could establish prior claims, they would be entitled to hunt and trap in these parks, an exception specific to Alaska. I had learned much about the region's topography from an Inupiaq elder in Alatna, a village north of the Arctic Circle. When I visited for the first time, I had found his mudroom cluttered with the implements of a bush life. There were slumping hip waders, foul weather gear, snowmachine parts, dip nets, a shotgun, beaver skin mittens dangling from a nail, and a chainsaw with a chain that needed tightening. Two wolf pelts flowed from the rafters complete with tail, legs, ears, and muzzle. Before I knocked on the inner door, I had stroked the silver-tipped fur. The eyeholes and the hides' steamrolled appearance had left me slightly unsettled, as did the landscape, muskeg and black spruce that hid grizzlies and mischievous spirits.

A dead beaver sprawled on the kitchen floor, half-skinned on a piece of cardboard, to keep the meat clean and blood off the linoleum. The elder asked me to sit. Before I unrolled my maps on the table, we snacked on jerked caribou we dipped in seal oil, a liquid-amber delicacy sent by relatives on the coast.

He pointed out the routes of his hunting and trapping expeditions. During the Depression, his forays had taken him farther north, way above timberline, to the snowy domes of the Brooks Range, and as far south as the willow-choked banks of the Yukon River. In the mountains and uplands, his semi-nomadic ancestors had hunted caribou and immaculate Dall's sheep for thousands of years, in friendly competition with packs of wolves. The meanders he drew on my maps with felt pens of various colors reflected the maze of animal ranges wildlife biologists chart on theirs. The elder's eyes took on a distant expression, as if he were reliving each mile on the trail. Reminiscence softened his crinkled, leathery face.

Other ethnographers who worked with Arctic hunters noted that, although these had never before seen a map, they could easily read one, recognizing *nuna*, "the land," even in its graphic abstraction. Before printed maps of the region existed, explorers elicited mental ones from the locals, who drew them by heart. Sketches the Danish adventurer Knud Rasmussen gathered in this way on his dogsled trip through the Northwest Passage impress with great detail. The landscape, larder and refuge for the spirit, had been fully internalized. The distortions also are telling. The Inuit depicted familiar settings, *their* bays, lakes, lagoons, and inlets in a scrimshaw based on travel and toil. The periphery, unknown coasts and plains, appeared vague, diminished in size and detail compared to the homeland. Women knew areas near the camps more intimately, their turf for rabbit snaring, berry picking, digging up roots. Conversely, men knew distant trade sites, passes, and portages, furbearers' itineraries, and the trails generations of caribou had inscribed in the tundra.

I also had read about tactile Inuit maps of the Greenland coastline; fashioned from driftwood, they could be "read" in one's pocket, upside-down, in wet and whiteout conditions or in polar darkness. Plotting the island's navigable fringe, the artifacts' indents and prows, inlets and capes of that sea-sculpted coast, ascend one side of this Inuit artifact and descend the other, as if North didn't matter. A man named Kuniit notched these lumps before his small, mobile band saw the first European, in the 1880s. In their simplicity the maps condense ingenuity, and touching the familiar objects like worry stones must have been reassuring to any storm-tossed kayaker.

Unknown to most of us, a palimpsest of collective memory precedes our own everywhere in North America. Accompanying Alaska Native elders on hunting and fishing trips, I found that each slough, each mountain pass, each falcon roost, or bear den told of a past that is also present. The landmarks and associated stories expressed philosophies about sharing and ownership, about conflict and community as much as they held knowledge passed down the generations. The maps, names, and stories focused the traditions of a culture whose identity resides in the land.

From early adulthood on I've shared the elders' peripatetic streak. In lieu of their guidance, maps and books fostered my

independence, inciting me to walk new terrain. Drop me anywhere with a map, and I can find the way home. I wish there
were similar aids for living my life, distillates that advise path-
ways from dream to goal. Maps also fed my imagination. Seeing
their contours I envisioned landforms and overarching patterns
and, like the writer I would soon become, I built inner worlds.

I had wanted to make this Alaska crossing for years. On
guided trips there never was time to explore all tempting vistas,
or routes the maps hinted at; clients demanded my attention,
and I couldn't ignore the tight schedule for reaching our destinations either. However, I could not take a whole summer off
for a private trip, as that was when I earned most of my income.
Beyond that, I would have needed a boat and new gear and to
pay pilots for food drops and my own charter to Joe Creek, the
starting point near the border. So I kept putting it off. Then, on
one backpacking trip to the Hulahula, our group encountered
a through-hiker at the airstrip where we awaited our plane. I
surprised him while he picked up a cache for the next leg of his
traverse. He was so used to being alone, so absorbed by what he
was doing, that he startled when I first spoke, though I'd tried
to avoid sneaking up, afraid he'd mistake me for a bear. Talking to this hiker, who was doing what I'd only kept dreaming
about, I realized he was no Superman, no Hugh Glass or Ernest
Shackleton. He was just a guy who had started to plan it and
then followed through.

I'd also postponed the traverse repeatedly because I thought I
had plenty of time. But perhaps I didn't. The fate of Judy, a client
on another Arctic backpacking trip served as a blunt reminder.
The petite teacher had fallen hard for the Brooks Range at our
first campsite, a mountain-cupped lake whose color transmuted
under the restless sun and clouds from quicksilver to pewter to
jade, like some celestial slideshow. She wanted to get funding to
return the next summer with students. At camp two days later,
she mentioned chest pains. She had not been injured or sick,

and I gave her generic painkillers, thinking she might have a strained muscle from her heavy pack. She seemed fine the rest of the hike. The following spring, my boss told me Judy had died two months after our trip. When she'd consulted a doctor about her lingering pain he had diagnosed lung cancer, inoperable.

Beholding the map set of my traverse, my eyes flick to the journey's beginning twenty miles from the Canadian border. I'd hiked east for a day, for a sense of completeness, to toe the line dividing what can't be divided—the hardest part of the trip, as 1,000 miles lay ahead in the other direction. I found none of the stone markers that cairn the cleared corridor between the two countries. Streams cross it without passports, as do snow geese and caribou, flowing forever between winter and summer ranges. Kin by custom and by blood but divided by politics, indigenous peoples dwell on each side. On my easternmost map sheet, Canada—"not us"—had been amputated, flush with the longitude grid. An old atlas of mine renders the neighbor pale gray, insubstantial. Invisible, that boundary, the longest straight line in the country, runs from Demarcation Point south to Mt. Saint Elias, where it jigs into the littoral of Alaska's panhandle; for nearly 700 miles it follows the 141st meridian west, one more filament of cartographic imagination.

In the heart of Gates of the Arctic, Anaktuvuk Pass, an enclave of 300 inland Eskimos, straddles the Continental Divide. On my map it's a cluster of flyspecks. The "Place of Caribou Droppings" rouses fond memories. I'd mailed myself a box of greasy goodies, one of six caches I'd arranged along the traverse, and devoured smoked oysters and salty potato chips sitting in the dirt lot of the trailer-size post office. The dinged pint of ice cream from the village store to me was worth four times the eight dollars I'd paid.

Following map contours with my feet, not my eyes, I quickly wised up to the cartographers' code. Bunched, chocolate-brown hairlines meant steep climbs or descents; "hedgehog" outlines promised abysmal swamps—could those be stylized tussocks? Robin-egg blue stood for lakes, ponds, and rivers or, finely striated, for snowfields and glaciers; the same hue spelled the same substance, also: wet crossings, creek-side coffee breaks, slippery footing. Black airplane icons, lettering, or cabin-squares announced human presence, which I could do without. Still, my throat tightened when I saw the glint of the tube that siphons a nation's lifeblood from Prudhoe Bay to Valdez. I was gazing down from a notch in the Philip Smith Mountains, the westernmost range of the refuge. I knew then that, short of an accident, I could finish this trek, step by step and one day at a time. Roughly two thirds of the hiking segment now lay behind me, and, strangely, the silvery thread in the distance conjured the comforts of civilization, and my former home Fairbanks, near that same pipeline.

I had not fully anticipated the hardships along the way. Maps are for fantasizing. Printed crisply on paper, they encapsulate space and time. Reality is measured in elevation-feet lost and gained, in tough miles on the ground. It should have been obvious. The Brooks Range cannot be found on even the best of maps. True places never are, Melville thought.

What my USGS quadrangles fail to show: tussocks, the mopheaded, knee-high wigs of vegetation that taxed my knees, ankles, and spirit; the section of Ekokpuk Creek, the worst bushwhacking of the trip, not even hinted at by the usual mint green patches on the map; the depth of streams I had forded with hiking poles vibrating in the current; the veils of mosquitoes that shadowed me eager for a meal; the opportunistic grizzlies that circled downwind for a rank whiff of me (which normally sent them bolting). Though I did not mark wolf encounters on these sheets, I can to this day pinpoint each one to within half a mile, can resurrect each one from memory scraps even without my dense notes. The maps do not hold the steel taste of spring water so cold it induced ice-cream headaches. They excise the perfume of crushed heather or Labrador tea, the soughing of breezes, falcon shrieks, and the tang of August blueberries. They omit the fog that blotted out Peregrine Pass, the gusting in the Noatak valley, the rain that soaked me for thirty consecutive days. They can never convey the magic of puppy-eyed seals bobbing near my boat, of cranes' pterodactyl calls echoing off the still river's skin. Nor do they include the small corner of the map quadrangle I chose not to buy, out of thrift, which, out there, sent me into a cursing and scouting frenzy. You don't find in them either the image of me afterward, reduced by twenty-five pounds yet refined, somehow, to my essence. Together with those pounds, mental dross and routines had been stripped away. Six hundred miles walking and 400 rowing the Noatak River, all solo, had reopened my eyes to nature's small, quiet wonders.

In addition to choices, the maps with my entries on them offer advice: *seize the day*. I regard the tiny black cross I drew at "Judy's Lake," where, thinking of her, I again camped. She had become part of that landscape, and that lake a reference point in a personal, storied geography.

The blue swath on my westernmost map—the Bering Strait, endpoint of the traverse—stretches south to the shores of my hometown Nome, a more permanent basecamp of sorts. Roughly 100 miles from the Arctic Circle, on the continent's edge, on the western prow of Alaska and the brink of tomorrow (with only a short plane ride to the dateline), I still feel close there to the Brooks Range, locus of my desire. Snowmelt from its south faces courses down rivers to lap at my doorstep. Fed by the streams draining north, the Beaufort Sea seamlessly blends with the Bering Sea, which heaves 200 yards outside my living room window. There are no topographic margins, I realize once again. Unlike a two-dimensional sphere, a Mercator projection, Earth has no here or there, no beginning or end. The center is everywhere. More so than the maps arrayed in my living room, the world they bring to us is connected.

Convergences

> Everything is flowing—going somewhere, animals and so-called lifeless rocks as well as water.
>
> —JOHN MUIR, *My First Summer in the Sierra* (1911)

ENCOUNTERS WITH WILDLIFE can feel like payback for karmic points earned and keep some of us buzzing for days. Perhaps more than in its weather or plants, the land's life force concentrates in its creatures, sharpened to poignancy, similar but foreign enough to our own to be captivating. To a few people it, or a thing closely related to it, becomes audible. A fellow wilderness guide describes it as a low frequency sound, "like a didgeridoo," which she has come to expect in certain places and greets as an old friend. Of course, the humming just might be tinnitus, or our mind wanting to hear something, anything, beyond sub-polar silence.

One fall day on a Canning River raft trip I guided, at the western boundary of the Arctic National Wildlife Refuge, will always remain special to the trip's participants for what the land offered up without asking for anything but our attention.

Sipping coffee in the morning's quiet, looking south from the top of the bluff where we had pitched our tents, I noticed a white blob on the bench below muscling toward camp. I did not believe my eyes. A polar bear! The clients popped from their nylon cocoons like ground squirrels from their burrows when I alerted them—one clad in boxer shorts and a down jacket. My co-guide Cyn insisted on getting the shotgun from its waterproof sleeve by my tent. We stood and watched the bear sniff and root around. To the marine mammal-dependent carnivore (the largest on land), ground squirrels, foxes, or birds could have been the only morsels of interest there. But as mere flashes in its metabolic pan, they would never provide enough calories for this blubber-burning powerhouse.

The bear's wedge head swung on its pendulous neck, snake-like, gauging god-knows-what. Thirty miles from the coast, radiant against heather and willows, the bear looked more displaced than it would have in a zoo. The previous year, sea ice—a haul-out for seals and hunting platform for the bears—had shrunk to the third-lowest extent on record. Hunger or curiosity could have driven the bear this far inland. It appeared healthy and fat, but if the spring ice had broken up early again, it would be in for a long fast.

In the spring of 2008, Native hunters had killed a polar bear near Fort Yukon, 250 miles south of the Beaufort Sea coast. Its inland excursion was the longest ever recorded for an Alaska polar bear. Normally at that time of year the animals would be ambushing seals on the sea ice. I only found out after our trip that our sighting qualified as the farthest inland sighting of *Ursus maritimus* in the Arctic Refuge. In 2011, a scientific study reported a polar bear marathon feat. A GPS-collared female with her yearling cub had swum 426 miles, from east of Barrow to near the Canadian border, across the Beaufort Sea. In search of an ice floe on which to rest, she spent nine days straight in barely-above-freezing-temperature water. Her cub did not survive. Clearly, as far as northern species and their behavior go, we now should expect the unexpected.

Without a care in the world, the bear we'd been watching lay down for a nap halfway up the bluff's slope. What was there to fear?

We sat and kept our binoculars trained on the pile that could easily have been mistaken for a limestone boulder. Occasionally, the bear lifted its head to sample the air. We crouched downwind from it, and it remained unaware of our presence.

Before long, a golden eagle stroked past. Mobbed by some gulls but regal in its bearing, it scrutinized the bear, which did not wake up. Then another bright spot heading downstream caught my eye. A cub? But the gait was different, a trot with a mission more than an ambling, the mark of canine determination, not of the larger carnivore's easy opportunism. A scan with my glasses revealed a white wolf.

Animals congregating near us for no obvious reason leave us mystified and in awe, even more so when they are "charismatic" or rare. They represent connections we have lost, evoking lineages and life ways that once were familiar but now seem arcane. They appear as sudden emissaries, omens, or uncanny messengers, although most of us no longer speak their language. At our layover camp, tracks of caribou, wolves, moose, bears, foxes, and a wolverine had stamped the mudflats with the animals' hidden intentions. The day after, we had observed a black Arctic fox, a moose built like a bulldozer, and a peregrine striking a ptarmigan on the fly and passing it off to a juvenile bird, all within one hour. Animals even sought contact with us on occasion, mirroring our curiosity. Mew gulls escorted the rafts, screeching blue murder and sounding like rusty door hinges. Caribou high-stepped closer, curious, eyeing us nervously. I baited them onward by waving my paddle overhead. A red fox, nonnative like myself and likely to cannibalize its smaller Arctic cousins if it came upon them, investigated our dinner setup. Even in the continent's frugal margins, the paths of animals had changed. *We* had changed them by our mere presence.

Sure, there were explanations for such meetings, for the overlapping of agendas in space and time, or at least the beginnings of explanations. Caribou are known to be nosey, gulls and terns peckish about intruders. Mornings and evenings, mammals tend to be more active, avoiding mosquito peak times or heat, fueling up for a cold night or the day ahead. With their patchwork of habitats, rivers provide food and cover for predators and prey alike. Their corridors ease travel, funneling animals and humans from the boggy and lumpy tundra onto natural highways. In part, our encounters were signs of the land's seasonal abundance, the narrow window for blooming and birthing, maturing and mating, that winter too soon slams shut. We also had to account for selective perception, our minds' intense focusing. The more we yielded to our surroundings, and the better we learned to look and listen for signs and shed our civilization's blinders, the more animal sightings rewarded us. When our attention strayed to daydreams or to each other, wildlife must have slipped past unnoticed. Despite our desire, the landscape seemed lifeless for hours at a time and miles around. We frequently surveyed it from a hilltop or standing up in the rafts, finding no movement except in the river's slippage beneath scudding clouds. What orchestrated animate meanderings across this land? What tangled invisible paths at greater than random frequency? Did life attract more life, beyond caloric or reproductive incentives? Was there some animal magnetism, some orbiting of terrestrial bodies about which we knew nothing but which included us?

Shadowing the Porcupine Caribou Herd on their migration for a thousand miles, the writer and wildlife biologist Karsten Heuer heard a "guttural thrumming" at significant moments in the herd's migration. Low-frequency "infrasonic" exchanges across distances much greater than those bridged by ultrasounds have been documented for elephants and whales. Heuer believes the phenomenon he witnessed could be a key to understanding communication that orchestrates the Porcupine Herd's moves and even transcends species boundaries. This strongly resonates with the beliefs of Gwich'in Indian hunters who, regarding caribou as distant kin, claim that they can converse with them.

Unconcerned with attempts to make sense of it all, fully present instead *here* and *now*, the wolf approached the sleeping bear. Casting sideways glances and giving it a wide berth of respect, it then sauntered over a ridge, out of sight but already etched into memory.

Because the bear was not moving much and posed no immediate threat, I had breakfast and broke down my tent. Then I acted as lookout while the rest of our group took their turn and loaded the rafts, screened by the bluff and prevailing wind. As I contemplated Sleeping Beauty with some voyeuristic unease, I realized once again that, out there, who spots whom first amounts to a matter of safety. Vision, hearing, and sense of smell have been refined to various degrees in the tundra's denizens to ensure survival of the most sentient. Exposure and this landscape's spare natural soundtrack awaken instincts long dulled in us. Compelled by sudden unease, I once switched banks hiking along an Arctic creek, only to round a bend and rouse a bruin with her two cubs right where I would have been stepping. Another time, I noticed *Boykinia* spiking a slope. Knowing that the white flowers are catnip to grizzlies, I wondered if there were any close by. And lo, when I hollered, one popped from a ravine thick with alders I'd been about to cross.

Alert, we become fully, if at times frightfully, alive.

As if to drive home that point, a camouflaged couple we'd run into below the Marsh Fork confluence came floating around the bend. Velvety caribou antlers in the raft's bow attested to their prowess as hunters. But they drifted by with their bloody cargo, oblivious to the predator outside their field of vision that had just bumped them to a lower rank on the food chain. I shuddered to think how often I had courted disaster unknow-ingly, like this.

When we shoved into the current a few hours after the initial sighting, the bear was up and moving again, sniffing and paw-ing through bushes on the bench. We snuck away like thieves, enriched by an encounter that luckily stressed none of the par-ties involved.

Over the next fifteen miles, our course intersected with that of a northern harrier, a rough-legged hawk, more peregrines, and low-flying, yammering loons. Another Arctic fox popped from between tussocks and then sat on its haunches with erect ears, intrigued by the bipedal transients.

Hours later, a tundra airstrip and a water flow gauge perched on a terrace on river right announced the end of our journey. They were the first manmade structures we had seen since we had launched a week before.

After a dinner upgraded by fresh grayling and salmon-red char, I dumped dishwater down the cutbank, scattering ground squirrels that had staked out riverfront property by tunneling below its lip. Straightening up, I faced a grizzly snuffling along the opposite shore. As we were gathering to keep tabs on its progress, furtive movement on our side caught my eye. Some dark troll momentarily rose on its hind legs for a better view of us. *Bear cub*, my thoughts clicked into the familiar groove; but Cyn correctly identified the creature: "It's a wolverine!" Loping toward us on flat feet, it stopped repeatedly, as if considering a dare. This allowed us to check the bushy tail, burly legs, and brawler's face characteristic of one of the North's most elusive animals. I stared in disbelief until my eyes watered. This was only my second face-to-snout with this weasel on steroids, and the first time, in Denali, it had been a mere glimpse. At roughly a hundred yards, the wolverine hesitated. Deciding that it had crossed some kind of threshold, it bolted, jumped into the river, and tread water till it reached the other side. Onshore, it shook its backlit coat, sending a burst of droplets flying in all directions. By then, the bear had bedded down for the evening. The wolverine continued upstream where it spied the bear. Like its wolf counterpart before, it detoured around the shaggy, sleeping mound. Then it clawed from the gravel bar up onto a bench and vanished behind a rise.

What a strange variation of a theme, like an *Animal Planet* rerun with a different cast. But to capture scenes like the ones we had witnessed in a single day, a documentary film crew would have to spend weeks or even months in the wilds.

Sunset had turned the northwestern horizon into a garish smear. A string of geese sailed right through it, black cutouts pulled by instinct to their fall staging grounds near Beaufort Lagoon. The river shone gunmetal blue, braiding and unbraiding into its delta, enticing us to carry on. Struck by oblique rays, sea ice glowed in the distance. The bear was still snoozing. When it got too dark to make out its shape, the clients crawled into their tents, trusting in our arsenal of pots and pans, pepper spray, and assorted firearms.

As evening river sounds will, the Canning's monologue made me pensive. In my fifty-two years on the planet, much of them spent in the backcountry, I had never seen a federally endangered species. This summer, I had seen two, the polar bear and a passel of humpback chubs in the Grand Canyon. I wondered if the odds simply increased as more animals ended up on that shameful list, or if, on some subconscious level, I sought out the rare and the blighted before they could disappear. The fact that my clients essentially funded my wildlife viewing and that the pollution I left in my wake possibly outweighed any awareness I hoped to instill further complicated matters. But I consoled myself with the thought that remaining childless was the biggest contribution I could make to preserve Earth. The lifetime carbon footprint of one offspring by itself would equal emissions from over 600 transatlantic flights. Despite flying north every year, I still had some miles to spare.

"A few recovered species don't compensate for the lost company of great beasts," the marine biologist Carl Safina writes. Sadly, he's right. But here there still were some wildlings, and we in their company, finding a measure of peace in these seamless days on the river. I knew that whenever the refuge played big in the media, because yet another attack on it was being launched, more visitors came. Many with whom I spoke confessed that they wanted to see this place while there was still time; a refuge for animals, we needed it just as badly. What we all felt, I'd like to believe, was a mixture of helplessness, guilt, and regret rather than morbid, rubbernecking curiosity. Like conscientious criminals, we were drawn to the scene of the crime, witnesses and perpetrators rolled into one, forever haunted by our deeds and sins of omission. Perhaps, in the great beasts' presence, we were hoping to somehow be forgiven.

Before I turned in, the realities of our streamside world dissolved into those of another, one by then almost forgotten. To the north, near the coast, orange gas flares and red strobes turned the night into a mad carnival. Flames split, fused and twitched in the crystalline air like some live alien thing. They spelled the undoing of everything we had experienced this past week. They proclaimed the place where sanctuary yielded to busyness, where extraction passed for production, where the earth and its creatures took second billing. They hawked the stuff that became our gear and got us to the river: Prudhoe Bay crude.

Least Force Necessary

THERE ARE THRESHOLDS we cross that leave us profoundly, irrevocably changed. They do not have to appear momentous, like an ocean, a border, a mountain range but can seem rather commonplace—a traffic sign, envelope, door of a home. We may not even be aware of facing one as we approach. I'm not saying this was one of the big ones. But I can't say either yet that it wasn't.

The moment I step up onto the tundra bench I realize my mistake. I forgot to shout "Hey bear!" like I normally do when beaching the raft, to avoid nasty surprises.

Right now, this slip of attention could get me killed.

Not twenty yards away, a grizzly stands up in the grass, fixing me in the crossfire of its stare. Next to it, two furballs, jolly as piglets: cubs. It's a worst-case scenario come to life.

What a mess. I have two clients on a beach upstream, one wet and fiercely shivering—luckily, he was able to swim ashore after flipping in this no-brainer rapid. I have his paddle, which I fished from the current after chasing it in the "mother ship," the big baggage raft. I don't have his $1,200 packraft (think six-foot-long synthetic donut, but rubber and elliptic, with a membrane-thin floor); that lies wedged into the rock garden on the Hulahula River's far side. Nor do I have the pump-action shotgun, which I left strapped on top of the load in my haste to hike back to my packrafters and unravel this snarl.

Overall, I don't like bringing guns. We're in the bears' home and it is impolite to shoot the host. But the company I work for requires its guides to carry firearms, and clients are more relaxed when we do. Personally, I prefer the least amount of force necessary to deter nosey or grumpy or pesky bruins, deploying a long-tested, effective escalation of choices. First, whistles, to make our presence known in brushy country (like the bright orange one tied to my life vest, the one I should have blown upon landing). Then pots and pans to bang together and thereby claim our turf with sound. And, most formidably, "pepper spray": a potent chemical aerosol pressurized in a can. It's the last-ditch of self-defense, also used by women and policemen in urban face-offs.

I am a staunch believer in bear spray. No serious harm has come to anyone who has used it properly in a bear attack. People with rifles or revolvers, on the other hand, have been maimed or killed, because a wounded bear is more dangerous than one that's only pissed off. We therefore weigh each of the slender black spray cans before the season starts to see if they're full. I keep mine in a side pocket of my pants, for quick access. However, as we caution everyone before each trip, your best survival tool is your brain.

Right now mine seems to be stuck after firing that mental blank when I stepped onto the beach. But reptilian reflexes take over. My arms go up. I mumble appeasement, apology. My legs move backwards, taking me down the bench to the rocky foreshore. I hope the bear won't follow.

She does. Like a hellhound charging after a fallen soul, she rumbles in my direction, a boulder trundling downhill. She's on all fours, bulked-up, center of gravity close to the ground in combat mode. Her ears are pinned back against her skull—a sign of her mood and to protect them from being bitten. As if I would.

In a motion that would do a gunslinger proud, I reach into my pocket, whip out the bear spray, thumb off the safety, and aim. Perhaps she is huffing, growling, chomping her jaws—I couldn't say. My focus has shrunk to needlepoint vision.

I already am wearing her mark, a paw print tattooed on my thigh. Down in Tucson, twenty-some years ago, cooped up in a ranch job, I tried to invoke wildness with this ink-stencil totem. I've had a bearish streak since childhood, bearish moods and manners combined with a blockhead that only worsens as I age. If you've seen bachelor bears out and about after six months of denning, you know what I mean. My hair is gray now; I could pass for a silvertip. But my beard, though bushy, is only a shadow of grizzly hirsuteness, and my sense of the land pales next to theirs. I regret not speaking their language, not knowing what they dream about in the winter. I rate my trips by how many bears we encounter. Still, smitten with them for decades, I don't want to be smitten *by* one.

But what I want or don't want does not matter right now. Chaos is calling the shots.

I am counting on her bluffing, that she will abort the charge at the last instant to test my resolve and send a blunt message: *Leave my cubs alone.* They say that most bear charges are mock charges, and I've weathered my share. If you run, bears will hunt you down. Standing your ground, though, is easier said than done. Every fiber in your body twitches to flee or curl up like a fetus. Experts "recommend" the prenatal position when a bear is upon you, to protect your vital organs, and no image better conveys your vulnerability under such circumstances than that naked, blind, unborn worm.

This really is happening, I realize, as she crosses the invisible line that would normally stop or deflect her. It is time to loose a red-pepper cloud. I press the can's trigger and, with a dragon's hiss, a burning jet hits the bear squarely in the face. She veers off less than ten feet from me.

No! The can is empty. I pushed down the trigger too long instead of giving one short, fell blast. Now I'm left without reserve. But it seemed too brief. *Did they actually weigh this can before sending it out on the trip?*

Sure enough, the bear, as if sensing my dilemma, turns the dodge into a fluid loop. She wheels about on her hindquarters, resuming the attack. I'm getting a bad case of déjà vu from this second round.

It takes longer to tell this than it did to play out, but as it's happening I sense time's elasticity, the trippy, simultaneous squashing and stretching of seconds that rides on adrenaline and speed-warps reality. I stand strangely removed, an impartial witness to my own demise.

Some people experience flashbacks; their whole history unspools before their mind's eye like a time-lapse film. External motion congeals, except for your own movements, and you have all the time in the world to react. Maybe you won't. You certainly *don't* have all the time in the world. The quickening is also a slowing-down. The ultimate quickening can be complete standstill: the cessation of you.

I am not a religious person; yet in situations like these, pledges are made, bargains struck, conversions affected. Souls alchemize in the crucible of fear. When we witness death, in nature or elsewhere, we confront it indirectly, because it is not our own. With your own life at stake, stoic poise evaporates in a flash.

To this day, I don't know exactly what happened next. I don't know if the soles of my hip waders slipped on algae-slick cobbles or if some archaic memory, some biological godhead, commanded me to lie down.

The bear has left, or so I'd like to believe, still lying on the ground. I feel no pain. In fact, I have not even been touched, I think. I don't know how close she came. Perhaps my eyes were shut. Carefully, without moving much, I scan the surroundings. Some people have been savaged, a few repeatedly, after standing too soon with a mad grizzly still hanging around.

I sit up, expecting deformity, blood, spilling guts. Soldiers and accident casualties can suffer short-term amnesia, and sometimes the opioid rush in their system masks even the pain of amputation.

But there's no blood. Nothing. I'm untouched. And the bear has skedaddled, cubs in her wake. I still cannot believe my luck.

With the threat to her young neutralized, she chose not to risk injury from this thing on the ground that had wielded some kind of stinger. In this hardscrabble place, health and survival are too precious to wager on a bet already won.

I take a few minutes to collect myself on the bow of the raft. My knees are like Jell-O—I can't even stand. Questions flit through my mind, like the proverbial sparrow, flying from darkness into the hall's light to exit again, too soon, into the night. Would my life jacket have absorbed some of this bear's anger? Would it have prolonged my life? Would my packrafters have been okay without me? I didn't even show them how to use the satellite phone to call for help; I never thought I might be the one who'd be helpless out here.

Oh shit! The clients. What if she rampaged upstream, tearing into them as they waited for me by the river's edge?

With the shotgun unsheathed, I lope through widely spaced willows, my heart thumping, whether still or again, I couldn't say.

I find them exactly where I last saw them and assess their physical state, as I just did my own. They look fine, a bit bored and shivery and then wide-eyed when they see me running toward them with a drawn weapon. The one who flipped his packraft would later tell me he'd worried I'd shoot him because he had messed up his run.

"Where did she go?" I bark, still in overdrive.

"Who?"

"Who? Who?! The bear that almost killed me!"

They never saw her. She must have circled wide, crossing the river farther upstream. When I search the bench by my raft after filling them in on the details, I find, as I thought I would, paw prints and fresh dung trailing upstream.

Back at base, my boss put the empty bear-spray can up on our warehouse "wall of shame," with my name and the date penned next to it, where it now hangs together with melted forks, broken paddles, bent tent poles, and a dirt-plugged shotgun barrel that had exploded when the guide pulled the trigger. But I felt no shame in my surviving and was not yet ready to chuckle at it.

I've been mulling "fate" much since that day. Is it mere chance? What were the odds that my carelessness would co-incide with the presence of a foraging mother bear? Of all the riverbanks in the refuge, why this one? Does your number come up in some perverse lottery by cumulative probability, by too many days spent exposed to the wilds? Being at the wrong place at the wrong time is part of bad luck. Mistakes in volatile situations then can be the timber that breaks your back, your avoidable contribution to disaster. If fate flows from character, as my line of work and enthusiasms do, then my run-in on the Hulahula was inevitable.

I can't fully attribute this bear's restraint to her sense of self-preservation, to wanting to avoid injury, or to her concern for her cubs. I prefer to believe, no doubt naively, that on some level I mattered to her, that she spared me out of compassion. I admire, perhaps even love her for not using more force to remove a perceived threat, especially given the harshness of her existence. Yes, "love," the big scary, overused, underused, clichéd word. But I have no other label for what washed through me then as it does now. Empathy mixed with gratitude approximates the emotion. Call it Stockholm syndrome or anthropocentric projection if you must. Unarguably, she left intact my violable self, at least its physical aspect. I would have been an easy kill, but she kindly passed when she could have battered, a force majeure in a pelt.

In this context, I cannot stop thinking about stuff that daily percolates through the news, about police brutality, our war on countries, on terror, on drugs, about imprisonment, rioting, eco-sabotage or other forms of civil disobedience, or even about our day-to-day "non-political" dealings with each other. When words or threats fail, pepper spray could do the job of bullets. Embargos could replace bombs. Like myself, the victims will be grateful, the cost to society less.

Perhaps we can learn from wild animals, or in some other way, to apply the least force necessary, responses appropriate to each transgression, each conflict. And perhaps the practice of killing "trouble bears," those that keep raiding garbage cans or have sampled human flesh, is not sound management but rather Old Testament retribution. Killing the "perp" doesn't bring back the dead or ease the survivors' pain. But they say preying bears acquire a taste for it and sometimes seek more.

To pack or not to pack in the backcountry—I struggle with that also. I have used a shotgun and was glad to have it. On the next trip I guided, we unknowingly camped near a protein bonanza on the Noatak River. We found out that salmon were spawning in a tributary about a mile upstream only after a Park Service plane landed on our gravel bar and the ranger opened with, "Did you guys bring a gun?"

Nerves frayed during the next two days. Bears showed up above and below camp exactly at mealtimes, as if in sync with our appetites, dragging ripe fish from the shallows. Some came so close we could hear them crunch spines and heads. Pots and pans did not impress that lot. Warning shots I fired when they drifted into our perimeter barely fazed them, but the clients looked pale. One monstrous, humped male materialized from the brush beside the latrine. Even after he'd sauntered off, I escorted a client whom nature was calling there, shotgun at the ready. I hardly slept for two nights and ran low on ammunition before the bush plane picked us up. I've never been happier to see the Noatak's aquamarine bends shrink behind a cockpit window.

I think of her sometimes, or rather, quite often, the one that spared me on the Hulahula: out there, under the midnight sun, drifting through crimson fall-heather, hiding in coastal fog, weary, horny, grouchy, content, pot-bellied or bony, digging her den, grubbing for roots, defying boars, or birthing more twins—hoping that she has not met an untimely end. I think of "her" not of "that bear" as if I really knew her. I'm not alone in this. Others who've been less lucky but survived feel the same way. I am bound to her not by friendship or blood or compassion, but by black blazing terror. Our bond can only be severed by death, hers or mine.

Gossamer Gold

I STEP FROM THE TUNDRA into an alder thicket like a blind man off a curb into rush hour traffic. Although it is quiet in here, except for the whine of mosquitos, my hackles rise. *Was that a branch snapping up ahead?*

In summery Nome, when the ocean's horizon blushes with midnight sun and shadows grow long and lean, this is one place you don't want to be: dense brush where grizzly bears feed or nap and don't like being surprised. Unfortunately, this is also where Nome's other gold, muskox underwool, can be found. To relieve their June itch, shucking their shag to prevent overheating, muskoxen take to the bushes where branches and trunks strip them of their winter insulation. The dark humps you glimpse now and again in the clearings can belong to one or the other kind of bruiser.

The gossamer fleece, which the Natives call *qiviut*, is eight times warmer than sheep's wool, keeping muskoxen cozy at fifty below. Ranging from off-white to beige, smoke-gray, and chocolate-brown, it is lustrous, soft as baby breath, and sells in stores for hard cash, 100 dollars per spun ounce. Wet feet or bug bites seem a small price to pay for such riches. As browsers, muskoxen seek thickets that clog creek beds and ditches, depressions into which melting permafrost drains; as suckers of heat-generating life, mosquitos seek the same windless spots on their sorties.

Propelled by my forager genes, I carefully follow a trail of dung pellets and crushed vegetation; silky hunks and skeins snagged on branches are flagging the mother lode: a foot-wide mop, like a badly made wig. I am poised, alert, and fully alive, in tune with my inner predator. Yet with all the adrenaline coursing, this is still not considered a "masculine" pastime here. Real men go out and *shoot* the beast with the prizefighter physique, though I hear it's as challenging as dynamiting fish in a barrel. The introduction of firearms by Yankee whalers at the end of the nineteenth century quickly extinguished muskoxen in Alaska's Arctic. They just let you walk up close, and if they feel threatened, line up in a bulwark of curved, embossed horns in front of their calves. Marksmen can fell them one by one, whole groups facing death bison-like, with the composure of statues. Several herds have been loitering around Nome in recent summers, wildlife officials say, to avoid bears. Hiding among us, as it were, as hunting them close to town is illegal. Near the AC Value Center store, they rest and digest, or play King of the Hill on an outcrop that dirt-bikers also love to shred. But wool gathered there is no good; it's dusty and matted like dreadlocks from being trampled. It would be much easier to post an ad at our online exchange site, Nome Announce, or the grocery store, and buy a whole hide from a Nimrod. Then I, or my wife, could comb out the fur, separating the *qiviut* from the unwanted coarse guard hair.

My wife Melissa—we got married recently, in a bare-bones ceremony at the courthouse after grabbing a witness at the post office—this is for her really more than for myself. She is a "wildcrafter," turning the land's bounty into various products. Increasingly popular in the Pacific Northwest where ecosystems are generous and in rural Alaska where supply always has been an issue, wildcrafting is fashionable once again, bookend to subsistence hunting or paleo-diets. On our windowsill sit Mason jars with dark alchemic fluids, homemade lichen dyes for this kind of wool. Melissa has an Inupiaq woman-friend with whom she picks stinkweed and arnica for cosmetics and creams. One-gallon Ziplocs of berries are taxing our freezer, preserved for pies, sauces, and jams. Driving through town, my wife takes mental notes on the muskoxen's hangouts to track them the minute she gets off work; we've already missed this year's salmon run. (Competition is stiff. Wildcrafters always watch for cars pulled over on dirt roads.) She is teaching herself spinning with a hand spindle. Her output includes knitted smoke rings, cowls, hats, scarves, and shawls. *Qiviut* does not keep a shape well enough to be made into sweaters. It's more of a feminine fiber, fit for lacy designs, I am told.

My spouse, clearly, is hardwired for gathering; I, on the other hand, lack any inclination to hunt. But I cannot escape the "something for nothing" mindset, and being in nature brings its own rewards: a bird's nest cushioned with *qiviut*; white-headed ptarmigan flashing lipstick-red eyebrows; a weasel popping from its burrow like a furry Jack-in-a-box. And on a great day: bleating muskox calves or head-butting bulls. I get into the spirit of things, dream of sneaking up on them with a rake, and rid them of their burden, that downy, stifling discomfort. A win-win situation, I'd say. Collecting next to my wife, I indulge in some friendly competition. I once again feel the flush of our courtship, like a bowerbird or fish-bearing tern, when I offer my mate a plastic bag bulging with *qiviut*. She never was one for flowers.

One could callously justify muskox hunting as a form of pest control, as, drifting through town, the beefy haystacks sometimes gore sled dogs tied up in people's yards. Some locals fear letting small children play outside when the "muskies" visit. Did they not know this when they made bush Alaska their home? Others think muskoxen compete with reindeer or caribou, foods the locals favor. Wary of traffic hazards, Fish and Game wardens have posted inflatable grizzlies alongside Nome's runway, to deter the archaic ruminants; these sentries sport a chest patch drenched with bear urine repellent—sold through the Internet, as "Predator Pee"—to up the scare factor. All in vain. From a window seat, I've watched bovine trespassers clip the green margins during takeoff.

Riding my bike into town, I sometimes, too often, see muskox pelts rotting on the porches of people who don't make time for combing them out. In this place, taking voraciously from the land is an esteemed tradition. Gravel pits, tailings ponds, and rusty mining machinery scar the landscape, drab reminders of past glories. Wool picking might not be as manly as gold digging or reenacting Pleistocene slaughter, but it clothes the family. I cherish its quiet luxuries and the thought that this way, the beasts get to keep their hides.

The Sweet Smell of Home

A SPRIG FROM A CREOSOTE BUSH infuses the steam in our shower stall with notes of the western Grand Canyon: tarry, resinous, bitter but rich. More sudden than fossil or feather or driftwood burl on my desk, it conjures a dear place and time, jump-starting memory like satiny wildflowers chanced upon between the pages of a book. Call it scent nostalgia, aromatherapy for the homesick. Outside, Arctic winter prevails, with the dearth of smells symptomatic of that season's deprivations. There, the olfactory monotone of old snow still reigns. Vapors carry scent molecules that move more freely and in greater quantity in warm, humid rather than cold and dry air. But knowing these facts does not make such absences easier to bear.

Like signature sounds, the signature scents of different landscapes are a sadly neglected aspect of place. We take pictures, record seashores or birdsongs, but depend on the spoken or written word for the archiving of scents. Scents need the storyteller, the writer, to endure and have their praises sung.

We are predominantly visual beings, underestimating or taking for granted what the nose knows until a head cold leaves us not blind, not deaf, not mute, but—what? There is simply no word (or solace) that comes to mind, for impairment of smell. Moreover, our descriptions of scents lack refinement, perhaps suggesting disinterest, a focus elsewhere. A hierarchy of the senses also buttresses place names. Names derived from smell, such as Stinking Springs, are even more rare than those we get from hearing (Thunder River, etc.), which in turn are vastly outnumbered by those in visual shorthand.

A dearth of "smelltalk" characterizes some cultures more than others. A now extinct shrub inspired Native Hawaiians to coin the term "octopus fragrance" for the delicious orange-like scent of its flowers. This was synesthetic metaphor, as morning and evening exhalations slipped from the dense groves like that animal from its reef lair. The Jahai of the Malay Peninsula, have a dozen terms for *types* of smell. One category includes fresh blood, raw meat, mud, stagnant water, and even some species of toad. Most English speakers cannot differentiate toads by sight, or describe cinnamon scent beyond calling it "spicy." Mind you, English also contains spot-on words for types of smell: "earthy," "fishy," "citrusy," "gamey," and others. But this is about the average person's vocabulary not Joyce's or Thoreau's. Linguists speculate that, unlike our sanitized, odor-poor cityscapes, tropical rainforests foster olfactory fluency.

Something besides individual variation is at work here, some form of genetic impoverishment. As we evolved to lead urban lives that no longer require us to find food or anticipate natural dangers, our organs of perception atrophied. The myopic, or those with less keen noses no longer were weeded out. Roughly sixty percent of the genes associated with sense of smell now lie dormant in most humans, except only those still living close to ancestral hunter-gatherer ways.

For all that, olfaction is "the orphan cousin of senses," and like many who suffer neglect, it can be the most inappropriately attention-seeking one of the lot. Some smells, Diane Ackerman writes in *A Natural History of the Senses*, "detonate softly in our memory like poignant land mines." Others insinuate themselves in the margins of perception, chords of a vaguely familiar melody. Aftershocks from such charges of volatile chemicals can last a lifetime.

Unlike the rest of sensory input, scent data bypass the thalamus, flitting straight to the brain's centers for emotion, decision-making, memorization, and navigation, where they coalesce into "odor maps." Scents can transport us instantaneously in space or time. When I travel south to the desert from wintry Alaska in the stale interior of a jet, a pressurized climate bubble like those cored from a glacier, Phoenix enfolds me as soon as the cabin door opens, welcoming me with a cocktail of heady particulates to a different place as if to a different season.

After twenty-five years in the North and Southwest, I can tap into a file of place-specific odors and complementary memories: a dwarf lupine field in the Arctic Refuge, like wading knee-deep through a pond of perfume. Rain-drenched sage in upper Snake Gulch—mentholated, medicinal, balm for the soul. (Even more distant flashbacks, to childhood chest rubs.) Piney whiffs from Labrador tea crushed underfoot on the tundra. Sunbaked, lichen-encrusted scree near Abajo Peak's tree line, something like flint struck for sparks, or burned sulfur. Loamy river: froth-broth at Lava Falls Rapid. Peppery rabbit brush and butterscotch ponderosa bark. Cliffrose, bell-ringing to bees, redrock country's ambrosia. Strengthened by the memories as much as by earth's ingredients, I am deeply inhaling their essence, trying to safeguard each one. Rare scent specimens come from moist, luscious gorges such as the Grand Gulch, whispers of mystery incense I have otherwise only sampled in Guatemala's cathedrals.

At the opposite of spring's floral awakening lingers the rot of deciduous fall; the putrescence of stranded, spent salmon; the sweet stench of walrus or whale melting on Nome's driftwood beaches and of cattle floating through Dinosaur's Echo Park like obscene bagpipes, bloated, legs sticking out—corpse food for vultures, which relish a chemical most vile to humans.

Scents ground us in nature's cycles, in death and rejuvenation. They mark us emotionally, even physically: juniper campfire impregnates garments and hair. Piñon-pine sap anoints skin, as does fetid river muck, or mud glazed by the tides. A blend of sweat, leather, mesquite, manure, with an edge of horse piss to this day signifies one of life's detours, my desert years as a wrangler. When times were tough, I'd find comfort burying my nose in a dusty mane or neck. Wyoming on horseback was different. Mossy-damp. Fungal. Exuberant. Oilskin slickers, wet felt hats, wet tack.

Each scent of a treasured place to me evokes an embrace, a friendly hand on the shoulder at least. Except for the gunk hole of low-water "Lake Foul" and the Cordova cannery, which gives the entire town seal's breath, there is not a stinker in the bunch. A person made homeless by flood or wildfire, I'm sure, would disagree. Indisputably, the charcoal air tickling bronchia in Fairbanks most summers betrays the town's flammable setting as unambiguously as does the veiled view from College Hill. Even the reek of an outhouse, braided with skeins of cigarette smoke, fondly resurrects rustic life, my stint in a cabin in the black spruce there. (It weakened during cold snaps, when frost furred the walls with sparkling sequins.)

Our indwelling creates scentscapes as unique and distinct as a genome or fingerprint. A kind of accidental olfactory stake claiming of territory, family fug is composed of the soaps, lotions, foods, furniture, fuels, building materials, and plants, the perspirations and respirations of household members and their pets, "an almost infinite variety of combinations," in the writer Bernd Heinrich's estimate.

Biologists like him have long considered the geographic bouquet, a quilt of fragrances that clues some creatures' wayfinding.

Floral spoors guide butterflies to their food. Ants lay down scent trails for other ants to follow. Pigeons, petrels, honeybees, and possibly bears and mice use odor maps of their neighborhoods to return to den sites or nests.

An olfactory prompt by a beloved location, a waterfall in Utah's Wasatch Mountains fragrant with mosses and columbines, led a University of Wisconsin biologist to discover how salmon return to their birthplaces. Imprinted in their youth, the adults get reeled in by a stream's chemistry, the unique composition of their natal waters. Smell and taste, of course, overlap. To be tasted, a substance has to dissolve in a liquid, bonding with water molecules. To a forager, his diet must appear mythical or like a mental map, each food item bound to a place of origin with its congruent scent.

"For many animals, scent is the primary window to the world," Heinrich writes in *The Homing Instinct*. Its signs and signals orient us too. Our ancestors heeded the dinner bell of ripe or fermenting fruit. An airborne dash of decay could lead to a predator's kill. Scent still bestows survival advantages, as it did in our species' past. A few people can smell nearby grizzlies in brush, but I have to watch caribou's body language for reassurance. They can sniff out lichen under five feet of snow, and when they are at ease heads down and grazing, so am I. Traces of rotten egg warn of bad waterholes, acridness of conflagrations. In my hometown in Alaska's interior, I'd often detect forest fires before they visibly thickened the atmosphere.

Scents reveal the hidden as much as they recall the almost forgotten. Air like a damp blanket or dog's coat heralds rain in the desert; the chlorine sting of ozone forecasts alpine lightning strike; gaminess betrays out-of-sight caribou trekking upwind or sometimes hangs trailing in their wake; musk spells *skunk in the bushes* or *marmot close by*. The sea announced itself to me once at the end of a ten-day river trip in the Arctic through a breeze redolent of sex, before the first gull had winged in overhead.

Old-time Navajos believed that the skunk, "One With Stinking Urine," which always finds water with a nose that makes up for poor eyesight, also might lead you when you are lost. If you cannot follow any skunks or gulls, trust the reptilian part of your brain. In my proudest feat as an outdoorsman, I recognized a campsite by its scent alone. We were floating through Cataract Canyon, and the night was moonless, like a cave. Worn out from the heat and rapids, we wanted to stop at Dark Canyon for a few hours of sleep. I had hiked there before and remembered narcotic, night-blooming "moonflower" pillowing near its mouth. Before long, the white-trumpet blossoms broadcast their availability to the moth that pollinates them, and their location to me. Invisible tendrils ensnared our fleet of rafts. Sultry, with a hint of vanilla, the plant's come-on smacked of a tarted-up woman, too much of a good thing. Seduced by the promise of bedding down we stepped ashore, home even if just for one night.

Glossary

Anasazi ancestral culture of the Plateau region of northern Arizona and New Mexico and of southern Utah and Colorado, from ca. 100 CE to 1300. The Hopi and other Puebloan peoples descended from it

Athabaskans (northern) Native peoples of interior northern Canada and interior and south-central Alaska. Related to Navajos and Apaches ("southern Athabaskans")

bentonite clay beds formed by the decomposition of mudstone and shale, sedimentary rocks common in canyon country

BLM Bureau of Land Management (also known as "Bureau of Livestock and Mining" or "Bureau of Lonely Men"). A much-loathed federal agency that manages huge swaths of Western lands

bunny boots cold-weather, rubberized footwear developed by the military, inflatable for better insulation

buzzworm slang for rattlesnake

cairn rocks marking a route or a trail; from the Gaelic *carn*, "heap of stones." Cairns are also built for other purposes, e.g., as memorials

cheechako "tenderfoot" or "greenhorn;" from the Chinook jargon that became popular during the Klondike gold rush (1896–1899). Denotes Anglo novice miners in contrast with "Sourdoughs," old hands who carried their pancake starter everywhere (and smelled like it, too)

cutbank nearly vertical "step" or bluff formed by the erosion of riverbanks, often from claylike sediments

drybag rubberized bag to keep clothes dry on a river trip

drysuit rubberized coverall to keep boaters dry and warm

Dall's sheep (*Ovis dalli*) one of several North American wild sheep species; predominantly white and native to subarctic Alaska, the Yukon Territory, the western Northwest Territories, and central and northern British Columbia. Named for William Healey Dall, a naturalist who carried out meteorological observations in Alaska

ducky inflatable kayak for one or two people

eddy a river current running counter to the main current or an area of calm water, a good "parking" spot for watercraft

firn snow high on glaciers in granular form before it is compacted into ice

Hypalon a synthetic rubber known for its resistance to chemicals, extreme temperatures, and ultraviolet light (and to a degree, rocks). The main material used for building inflatable boats

Inupiaq language and cultural affiliation of northern Alaska Natives currently still known as "Eskimos;" the term has lately become controversial for its racist overtones

katsina or **kachina** any of a host of ancestral and natural spirits the Hopi Indians deify. Impersonated by masked dancers in religious ceremonies. Also the painted carved "dolls" of such spirits, now a popular collector's item

kicker slang for a boat's outboard motor

kuspuk parka of lightweight cloth (often calico), worn especially by Eskimo women and children in summer

Lake Foul Edward Abbey's name for the Colorado River's Glen Canyon Reservoir, which some call "Lake Powell"

Lower Forty-Eight Alaska vernacular for the forty-eight contiguous states of the Unites States. Also known as "stateside" or "Outside" (or sometimes, "America")

masa flour or dough made of dried, ground corn, used especially for tortillas

medial moraine center ridge of rock debris or "glacial drift," formed by the joining of two glaciers

midden refuse heap that yields clues about ancient civilizations (and about our own)

muskeg type of bog characterized by sphagnum mosses, sedge, and sometimes, stunted black spruce and tamarack trees

NPS National Park Service

Old Ephraim term popularized in the 1800s American West, referring to grizzly bears

permafrost perennially frozen underground soil layer in Arctic or subarctic regions that causes poor drainage of surface water

piñon pine common in the Southwest. In canyon country this often is *Pinus edulis*, the two-needle piñon. Literally, "edible pine," for its nuts, which Native people harvest

pulk Scandinavian sled with a waist harness in which a skier can haul gear. Traditionally harnessed to draft reindeer

put-in where a river trip launches. This is not always a built concrete boat ramp

silvertip blond grizzly with hair ends that highlight its pelt. One of many brown bear color variants

slickrock smooth bedrock or rock formation in the desert Southwest. Often consists of sandstone, sometimes limestone. Not necessarily "slick" (except when it snows or rains)

snowmachine Alaska vernacular for snowmobile or skidoo

subarctic subpolar; refers to the region immediately south of the Arctic Circle

taiga the coniferous subarctic or "boreal" forests that cover vast areas of northern North America and Eurasia (from a Russian word of Mongolian origin)

takeout where a river trip ends, rafts are deflated, and boats loaded. Often situated near a parking lot and in rural Alaska, a gravel airstrip

Tonto Platform broad terrace about halfway between the river and rim, one of the Grand Canyon's most dramatic geologic features. It consists of layers of Tapeats Sandstone atop the inner canyon's tough granite and schist, and a trail skirts much of it on the south side

tussock tuft or clump of growing grass typical of poorly drained northern regions (i.e., muskeg)

USGS United States Geological Survey; government agency tasked with mapmaking and some scientific research

wadi channel of a watercourse that is dry except during brief periods of rain or snowfall; from the Arabic *wādī*

Acknowledgments

These chapters first appeared in different form in the following publications:

"No Walk in the Park," "A River Now and Again" (as "Riding the Ephemeral"), "Dancing the Rain," and "The Last Fifteen Miles" in *Northern Arizona's Mountain Living Magazine*

"At Home in a Hole in the Rock" in *Sierra*

"Classroom with a View" in *National Parks*

"Confessions of a Cat Lover" and "Mating Dance Under the Midnight Sun" (as *"First Date"*) in *Hell's Half Mile: River Runners' Tales of Hilarity and Misadventure*

"So Long, Promised Land" and "Biking Cool" in *Inside/Outside Southwest*

"Blacktop Cuisine" in *Going Green: True Tales from Gleaners, Scavengers, and Dumpster Divers*

"Berry-Pickers and Earthmovers" in *Cirque*

"Tough Times on Denali" and *"Honeymoon for Three"* in *Alaska*

"Recovery" in *Snowy Egret*

"Marginalia" and "Notes from the Road to Bestellerdom" in *High Country News*

"Convergences" in *Canoe & Kayak*

"Marooned" in *Wild Moments: Adventures with Animals of the North*

"Least Force Necessary" in *Adventure Journal*

"Gossamer Gold" in *EarthLines*

About the Author

AN ANTHROPOLOGIST BY TRAINING, Michael Engelhard has worked as a potter, wrangler, army officer, ship's cook, university teacher, outdoor instructor, and wilderness guide. Among his homes he has counted an oven-hot bunkhouse in Moab, an unheated sauna near the Arctic Circle, a houseboat parked on a ranch in British Columbia, and a blue-tarp hut shaped like a Tootsie Roll on the banks of the Rio Grande. His greatest accomplishment has been a 1,000-mile solo traverse of Alaska's Arctic, from the Canadian border to the Bering Strait. He is the author of *Redrock Almanac* and *Where the Rain Children Sleep* and the editor of four collections of nature writing. His most recent book is *Ice Bear*, a cultural history of that Arctic icon. Still moving often, he lives in Fairbanks, Alaska again.

⸿HIRAETH PRESS

⸿Poetry is the language of the earth. This includes not only poems but the slow flap of a heron's wings across the sky, the lightning of its beak hunting in the shallow water; autumn leaves and the smooth course of water over stones and gravel. These, as much as poems, communicate the being and meaning of things. We strive to produce works of poetry, whether they are actual poems or nonfiction. We are passionate about poetry as a means of returning the human voice to the chorus of the wild.

www.hiraethpress.com

CPSIA information can be obtained
at www.ICGtesting.com
Printed in the USA
FFOW04n0939240217
32783FF